To all young children who love to
Count and play with numbers and shapes.
We want to encourage them to keep that
love and enthusiasm all the rest of their lives.

COUNTING ON MATH

Developing Math Skills with Young Children

by
Martha A. Hayes
and
Kathy Faggella

Art by
Kathy Faggella

FIRST TEACHER PRESS
First Teacher, Inc./Bridgeport, CT

 ISBN 0-9615005-9-X

Library of Congress Catalog Card Number 87-083550

Cover Design by Gene Krackehl; Illustration by Debby Dixler

Edited by Lisa Lyons Durkin

Typesetting and Layout: Michael Pearl

Manufactured in the United States of America

Published by First Teacher Press, First Teacher, Inc.
P.O. Box 29, 60 Main Street, Bridgeport, CT 06602

Distributed by: Gryphon House, Inc.

P.O. Box 275

Mt. Ranier, MD 20712

TABLE OF CONTENTS

TABLE OF CONTENTS

WE BELIEVE THAT

■ each child just naturally does in her daily life activities that adults consider mathematics.

■ our role, as adults, is to help each child recognize math situations in their activities and encourage the children to apply their knowledge and experiences to any problems that occur.

■ each child should experience the steps involved in the solving of problems in order to be able to apply them to a new situation that might be encountered.

■ each child should be given the opportunity to experience mathematical processes concretely at first in order to then be able to understand and do them abstractly.

■ each child needs to have the opportunity to talk through her solutions as she discusses the mathematical situations with other children and adults.

■ each child should have the opportunity to seek solutions to problems and respect should be shown for her solutions no matter what they are.

■ each child should gain a feeling of satisfaction and self-confidence from solving problems constructively.

OUR PHILOSOPHY

Children have been "doing math" since infancy.

Long before children take paper and pencil into hand to begin adding and subtracting columns of numbers, they have spent at least five or six years experiencing activities, relationships, and concepts that we call mathematics. Through infancy, toddlerhood, and the preschool years, they often have been working with real objects and solving their problems.

Problem solving is a skill that should be practiced and refined from infancy on. Children need to learn how, why, and where to acquire knowledge; then, how to use that information to solve problems. Parents provide opportunities both inside the home and out, and so do you, their teacher. Classrooms should make available many experiences and situations where children can reason and solve problems on their own. It is here, too, where the steps involved in certain types of solutions can be demonstrated. These steps become models for children to use later on as they work out their own solutions.

It is important to provide a large variety of math-related materials for children to explore freely.

One key to helping children develop mathematical skills is to provide a large quantity of varied materials that they can use and explore. By observing and handling objects, young children can begin to know the properties of the objects. For example, the more different types of balls young children play with, the more they realize that "ball" refers to something round. The more chances children have to come in contact with real objects—through all five senses—the more they notice that things are the same or different. They will also sense amounts, shapes, sizes, and patterns.

We believe that you have excellent opportunities to demonstrate the processes involved in formulating and solving problems in the various subcategories that are a part of a total mathematics program—all of which children will need in everyday situations. At the same time, we realize that we must provide some type of structured program that includes a balance of activities from the entire math field. We feel that the pertinent subcategories or areas for young children include the following: numbers, reasoning (logic), shapes (geometry), patterns, measurement, recording and using information (statistics and probability), higher-level thinking (algebra), estimating (mental math), and a knowledge of mathematical helps (calculators and computers).

A good math program includes a balance of activities from all math areas.

The structure of this program provides for an open, exploratory atmosphere that allows children to test out or experiment with many ways and many processes and eventually arrive at solutions. We also feel that it is important for children to talk through the processes and the solutions with their friends and classmates and a caring adult. Eventually, we know that children will come to understand that although there may be many ways to solve a problem, there are certain ways that are more commonly preferred.

CHILDREN AND MATH

It is important to include mathematical concepts in all areas of young children's lives.

"Mathematics" is a word that most young children probably never have used or even heard. Yet, they have been using aspects of it every day--they determine amounts, they use what they know about shapes when building, they sort by categories, they measure, they estimate, they figure out unknowns, and they problem solve. In their homes and at school, they have probably, however, not gone through a specified math curriculum so no one is sure that children have been exposed to or practiced the many areas involved in mathematics with the same regularity and degree. Nor are we sure that children know the best ways to use mathematics to solve problems that occur in their daily lives. This book has been developed to help adults and children become aware of mathematical areas or concepts that probably should be included in young children's lives so they can explore, investigate, and discover more about math. These are the areas that they will meet and have to absorb quickly when they enter school.

Math is numbers:

Mathematics is a science that deals with quantities and their measurement, their relationships, and their properties. These quantities are expressed in numbers or symbols that stand for those numbers. When young children deal with our number system, they are learning the oral or written symbols (numbers or numerals) that indicate quantity, they are counting, and they are sensing the order in which the symbols occur. Children are using their number knowledge when you make statements or ask questions similar to the following.
- ■ "How many?"
- ■ "Tell which one is first, next, and last."

Math is reasoning (logic):

The ability to use logic or to reason is essential for children when learning mathematics because they have to look at problems and figure out what is known, what the problem is, and what are ways of solving each problem. An essential part of the reasoning process is the ability to sort objects and ideas into groups so that conclusions can be reached about each whole group or about all or some of its members. Children are using their reasoning abilities when they hear statements or questions such as the following.
- ■ "Put the same kind of objects together in a group."
- ■ "What is the 'name' for this group?"

Math is shapes (geometry):

Because children live in a multi-dimensional real world, they must learn to use that part of mathematics that includes the study of shapes. With all areas of mathematics, it is very important that children work with concrete objects. Geometry is the one area, however, where it is absolutely essential that children see (visualize) and handle objects of the various shapes being discussed--both two- and three-dimensional. Young children need to experiment to find out what can be done with all the different shapes they encounter. Once children learn the names of various shapes, they can then be shown other objects and asked questions similar to the following.

- ■ "What shape is this object?"
- ■ "How do these shapes fit together?"

Math is patterns:

There are all different types of patterns in a child's mathematical world--the various number patterns (by 1s, 2s, 3s, 5s, 10s, and so on); the symmetrical division of two halves; the degree of difference along certain continuums such as from coldest to hottest, from smallest to largest; and the patterns with different sizes, shapes, and colors that children can copy, extend, or develop on their own.

Math is measurement:

Measurement is an area where children look at various items and use numbers and different types of measuring tools to give information about the size or amount of what is being studied or discussed. Children provide quantative information determined by measuring. An important and early part of measurement is having children make comparisons between actual concrete objects since they will be doing lots of estimating of size or amount in order to see what fits or how much should be used. Children use measurement when they are asked to respond to such questions as the following.

- ■ "Which object is taller or the tallest?"
- ■ "Is that object full or empty?"
- ■ "Which one of these things is the heavier or the heaviest?"

Math is reporting and using information (statistics):

Mathematics must be used with children in order for them to see the necessity for learning more about it. Mathematical information needs to be presented in simple and visual ways so that children can interpret it quickly and easily. An essential step in this is the collecting and organizing of data and the presentation of it in graphics, such as tables and graphs. Children at an early age can respond to simple types of graphs, especially pictographs and pie graphs. Children are using statistics when the group is asked questions such as the following.

- ■ "What do you think is the favorite (food, color) of our group?"
- ■ "How will we find out and then show what we have found out?"

Math is higher-level thinking (estimation, probability, algebra):

Since young children really are already using aspects of estimation, probability, and algebra in their daily lives and, since it is important to encourage children to do abstract thinking, various activities involving these areas have been included in this book. The activities will help children better understand the concepts as they apply them to actual, practical problem-solving situations. They will better prepare the children when the higher-level thinking processes involved in these areas are actually taught in later years. Children are using higher-level thinking when they are asked questions such as the following.

■ "What is your guess about how much will fit into this container?"

■ "Do you think five or six children will be able to play here?"

■ "What will the group probably want to do after snack?"

■ "How many different ways can you divide these six buttons?"

Math is problem solving:

There are certain steps that children can follow as they are faced with problems. They often, however, go off in all sorts of directions, and then, make "stabs in the dark" and are frustrated because satisfactory solutions do not occur. Young children can be introduced to some of the steps in problem solving at an early age so that there may be some type of organized effort in their attempts. Children are using some steps in problem solving when they are asked questions similar to the following.

■ "What do you need to think about in order to do this job?"

■ "What is wrong here and how will you fix it?"

■ "What must be done to solve this problem?"

HOW TO USE THIS BOOK

Counting on Math is a guide that gives information about mathematical concepts, and then, shows you how to encourage children to use and develop their mathematical abilities. We have provided discussions of various skill areas and suggested concrete activities and projects where young children can have experience using the processes of these different areas. The activities are centered around those themes that occur in most early learning and kindergarten centers. Children can see that mathematics can be applied in typical classroom and home situations--with real-life, concrete materials. You can use the suggestions as written or adapt them to your own situations.

Each chapter contains information and activities that enhance all or most of five specific mathematics areas: number, reasoning, shapes, patterns, and measurement. In addition, most chapters will have activities that deal with one or more following abstract thinking areas: reporting and using information (statistics), estimating, and higher-level thinking (algebra or probability). There are two project pages in each chapter that list, step-by-step, activities that reinforce one of the skills discussed on the page to its left. There are also problem-solving pages that can be reproduced and given to children. These are participatory pages that require children to do something on them or with them using one of the math areas that has been previously discussed. At the end of each chapter is a page entitled "Discovery Time" with suggestions for possible activities, materials, and questions that can be placed before the children so they can explore and experiment on their own. You only have to "set the stage" for children to create their own hands-on experiences in the different math areas.

On the project pages, the directions are given so that you will know what you need to do and what you can ask the children to do. We will tell you when a task is too difficult or too dangerous for a young child to do alone and when the child will probably need your assistance. However, you must be the final judge of what each child can do. Remember that safety is always the major concern.

Counting on Math can serve as a readiness book or as a catalyst for your class. Our suggested activities were written to benefit most young children. You will, however, want to personalize the problem-solving situations to meet the needs of your unique group. You will need to know how much of a math background each child has. Make children's work in mathematics enjoyable and nonthreatening. Give children lots of varied experiences. Remember that you should be interested in exposing children to various mathematical processes, but not worrying about the product or the exactness of what is done. Use this book, also, to assist you in planning other activities, projects, and games that will enable children to have more experiences with the different areas.

SKILLS REFERENCE CHART

X - Main Math Skill
O - Additional Math Skill

	NUMBER	LOGIC (CLASSIFICATION)	SHAPES	PATTERNS	MEASUREMENT	REPORTING INFORMATION	HIGHER-LEVEL THINKING	ESTIMATION
Count on Me (29)	X							
Print and Sort (31)		X						
Shaping a Scene (32-33)	O		X					
Sew a Shape (37)			X					
Mystery Patterns (39)		O		X				
Circus Train (40-41)		X	O					
Shadow Measuring (45)					X			
Kinds of Leaves (47)	O	O	O			X		
Necklace (48)		O		X				
Melting Race (51)	O	O			O			X
Snowball Counters (53)	O	O					X	
Frosty Shapes (54)			X					
Sand Casting (57)	X							
Spring Tallies (59)	O	O			X			
Planting a Garden (60)	O						X	
Blowing Bubble Shapes (63)			X					
Fruit Kabobs (65)	O	O		X				
Sand Printing (66-67)			O		X			
As Time Goes By (71)					X	X		
What Do You Like (73)	O	O						
Keep in Balance (74-75)	X				O			O
Guess a Color (79)	O							X
Straw Blowing (81)							X	
Wallpaper Borders (82-83)	O	O	O	X				
Birthday Party Book (87)	X							
Book of Shapes (89)			X					
Fun at the Lake (90-91)			X					
Home Base (95)	O				X			
City Planning (97)			O					X
Computers (98)		O						
Calculators (99)	O						O	
Balloon Clowns (103)		X	O		O			O
Folding Fun (105)				X				
Tally-Ho! (106-107)	O	O	O			X		

PRE-READING SKILLS REFERENCE CHART

Activity	Using Math Helps	Details	Comparison	Following Directions	Motor Development	Part to Whole	Color Relationships	Sequence
Count on Me (29)		✓		✓		✓		
Print and Sort (31)		✓	✓	✓				
Shaping a Scene (32-33)		✓	✓	✓	✓			
Sew a Shape (37)					✓			
Mystery Patterns (39)		✓	✓					✓
Circus Train (40-41)			✓	✓		✓		
Shadow Measuring (45)			✓		✓	✓		
Kinds of Leaves (47)		✓	✓					
Necklace (48)		✓	✓	✓	✓			✓
Melting Race (51)			✓					
Snowball Counters (53)		✓				✓		
Frosty Shapes (54)				✓	✓			
Sand Casting (57)				✓	✓			
Spring Tallies (59)		✓	✓					
Planting a Garden (60)				✓	✓		✓	
Blowing Bubble Shapes (63)								
Fruit Kabobs (65)		✓	✓	✓	✓		✓	✓
Sand Printing (66-67)		✓	✓					
As Time Goes By (71)			✓					✓
What Do You Like (73)			✓	✓				
Keep in Balance (74-75)			✓					
Guess a Color (79)			✓				✓	✓
Straw Blowing (81)		✓	✓	✓	✓		✓	
Wallpaper Borders (82-83)		✓	✓	✓	✓		✓	✓
Birthday Party Book (87)		✓		✓				✓
Book of Shapes (89)				✓				
Fun at the Lake: Play (90-91)		✓	✓	✓				
Home Base (95)				✓	✓			
City Planning (97)			✓			✓		
Computers (98)	✓	✓	✓	✓		✓		
Calculators (99)	✓	✓						
Balloon Clowns (103)					✓	✓		
Folding Fun (105)				✓	✓			
Tally-Ho! (106-107)		✓	✓			✓		

GETTING READY

As with any good teaching, preparation and organization are very important. When planning to emphasize mathematics skills, when you are including them as part of a theme discussion, or when they are inherently part of an area in the room, you must consider the following details:

- the space you will be using;
- the general equipment needed;
- the specific equipment needed;
- what specific abilities each of your children has;
- the specific concepts you want to emphasize or provide experiences with for your children;
- how you will provide children with problem-solving opportunities;
- how you and the children will participate in the process of problem solving and creative thinking together.

Following is more discussion of the mathematics areas including some of the specific concepts involved in each area, ways that you can provide more opportunities for learning, some of the excellent materials that can be used to enhance a child's experimentation with certain processes, and some tips that will make it possible for a child to better understand a process. Remember to make the most of what is readily available to you in your room and school and to adapt ideas to your own particular children and situations.

NUMBER

Children meet numbers long before they have learned how to count. They are able to cope with small amounts without knowing the names that have been assigned as the names for those amounts. What fun it is when they start using number words! That's the time to begin to clarify what is meant by a number name or to help them tell how many are in a group. How do you do that? By modeling techniques and then, letting children follow your lead.

1) Point to each object as you say its name.

2) Move each object from one group to another so that the items in the group being counted have been manipulated.

3) Help children note when asked "how many" are in a group that the answer is the name of the last item touched.

4) Start at the same position or side when discussing the position of different objects.

Help children learn about numbers by modeling techniques.

Children are doing several different processes when they are thinking about numbers. Among these are the following:

- Noting one-to-one relationships between groups (comparing)
- Deciding which groups have more or less in them
- Saying numbers in order
- Counting objects and finding out how many
- Seeing numbers on calendars and clocks
- Understanding positional words--"first," "next," "middle," "last"
- Understanding ordinal words--"first," "second," and so on
- Beginning to recognize and count money--pennies, nickels
- Moving groups of objects together and separating them (adding and subtracting)
- Dividing a whole object into parts (fractions)

When they deal with numbers, children are using different processes.

In your room, you want to provide lots of opportunities for children to count and, at a certain point, to see the symbols that stand for the numbers being said. They can count almost everything--from themselves to their body parts, crayons, buttons, rocks, dolls, blocks, objects in picture, seeds that are planted,days of the week, weeks in the month. As you see, children will count almost anything put in front of them. They need to do so in order to better understand and recognize quantities. (This is even more important than being able to rattle off numbers in order without knowing the amount that each number stands for. Children should be encouraged to count so that they do become familiar with the order of the number system and what object is in a certain position.) To provide readiness for adding and subtracting groups of objects and seeing the relationships between groups, children need lots of chances to form groups by joining objects together or by separating a group into parts and to talk about what is being done. By manipulating the concrete objects, children may begin to sense that there is a relationship between the processes of joining together and taking away or dividing into smaller groups.

Provide lots of opportunities for children to count and talk about numbers..

REASONING

At a very early age, children begin using this skill because they start to classify objects into different groups. As children do activities specifically designed to enhance their reasoning skills, they will begin to note details about objects, make comparisons between objects in a group, and then, sort them according to one or more distinctive features. It is important that the first type of sorting they do is with concrete objects for this enables them to transfer what they know about this skill to doing a more abstract activity--sorting pictures of objects that have similar attributes. Later on, they will graduate to sorting the words that stand for the concrete objects or pictures.

When they classify, children learn to note details, make comparisons, and sort objects

There are certain steps that you can follow in this sorting or classifying process so that the first tasks are very simple and then, the further tasks become more complicated. The tasks, described below, pertain to children who are sorting attribute blocks. These objects vary in only three different ways--color, shape, and size.

1) Find another block that is the same color as this one.

2) Point out all the blue shapes.

3) Sort out all the objects into groups so each group shows a different shape.

4) Look at the blocks and sort them so that the red squares are together and so that the blue circles are together.

5) Now that different sized blocks have been added, you will have to look carefully to find all the big blue triangles and the little red circles.

Children are doing several different processes when they are thinking about objects and the attributes of each one. Among these are the following:

■ Noting the details and comparing objects that appear together but may not belong to the same group

■ Realizing that any object may belong to more than one category and can be sorted by more than one attribute

■ Using and understanding the meaning of words such as "all," "some," "none," "every," "few," and "many"

Children practice reasoning when they put away doll clothes in specific drawers.

Besides sorting attribute blocks, children are using reasoning skills when they put doll clothes away on certain shelves or in different drawers, when they put the same type of groceries together on a shelf, when they sort leaves found on a nature walk by their shape or color, or when they name a large group, such as "Animals," and then, tell the names of kinds of animals or specific breeds that belong in that group.

Children will be using reasoning when they describe the features that tell them that a certain animal is a dog and that another animal is a bird.

SHAPES

In this area, children explore more of the "shapes" in the world around them. They learn about various two- and three-dimensional objects and the attributes that make each one a distinctive shape. As they play and have to make the various-shaped objects fit into their plans, they must consider the size, shape, or position of each object. It is this play which aids children's understanding of geometry because it allows them to be kinesthetically aware of each shape of the shapes.

■ Let children "feel" the edges.
■ Have children count the corners.
■ Encourage children to build with the shapes so that they have a sense of each shape's dimensions.
■ Help them demonstrate various positions where objects can be placed: in, out, above, below, next to, after, up, down.

Creative play aids children's understanding of geometry.

Children are using logic and comparison processes as they are thinking about the different shapes in the world. Among these are the following:

■ Examining and identifying some three-dimensional objects—spheres, cubes, blocks, cones, cylinders (You may want to use the names normally given to the two-dimensional shapes here so as not to confuse children.)
■ Finding out what these different three-dimensional objects can do or be used for
■ Examining and identifying some one- and two-dimensional shapes—circles, squares, rectangles, triangles
■ Seeing how the size and position of the shapes affects what can be done with them
■ Recognizing shapes when looking at everyday objects
■ Realizing that an object can be made up of more than one shape
■ Understanding that a geometric shape can be divided into other geometric shapes

Obviously, children are using their knowledge of shapes as they build with blocks, as they draw the shapes of objects, and as they build sculptures from clay, snow, or sand. When you encourage their creative play, you are helping them practice mathematical skills.

The ultimate goal in this area is to help children see mathematical patterns in the number system so that they can find shortcuts as they compute. For example, the multiplication tables follow patterns. Since this is very abstract, children need to start by visualizing concretely simple patterns and comparing the objects that are the members of the pattern. They, then, begin to sense that there is an order to the way the objects in the patterns appear. Several steps help children note patterns.
1. Have children copy a pattern by repeating the order below it.
2. Start the children by showing them which direction to go.
3. Help children describe the objects in a pattern and then, tell what object will come next using such attributes as color, size, or shape.
4. Have children extend the pattern with at least four or five examples.

Children use different math and thinking skills as they create or determine patterns.

Children are using several different mathematical and thinking skills as they are determining and creating patterns:
■ Comparing items and classifying details of each feature in the pattern
■ Noting that often the difference between two parts of a pattern is often the geometric shape of each one
■ Counting the parts of a pattern if it is an uneven pattern

There are other patterns that young children may experience concretely and then, discuss the degrees of difference. Examples of these patterns are displaying items that go from smallest to largest or tallest to shortest, or sensing the differences between the coldest and the hottest items.

Children can use attribute blocks when forming patterns. Also, they enjoy stringing various colors and shapes of beads to form patterns.

MEASUREMENT

Young children must practice looking at two or more items and comparing them.

This area is one that children have been using for much of their lives since they have been examining full and empty food dishes, pouring sand in containers, making buildings with blocks, and saying "more." Now, it is time to clarify terms so that children will better understand the different ways to measure and which type of measuring to do in a particular situation. It is important that children realize that it is possible to measure in a number of different ways—size, weight, time, height, weight, area, volume, temperature, money—and that in each instance, there is a certain vocabulary that will be used.

In *Counting on Math*, children will be doing two types of measuring—looking at two or more items and using comparatives to describe the sizes is one; looking at one item and describing it is the other. In the second type, children will be doing lots of estimating or guessing since the standard terms—inch, foot, yard, pounds, and so on—are too difficult forchildren to comprehend at this age. However, it is important for them to begin to understand and practice some of the aspects of measurement, such as:

■ Noting carefully the outer limits of what is begin measured

■ Being sure to know about some types of measuring tools and how they are used

■ Understanding that when comparing two items the suffix *er* is often added to the descriptive words; when comparing three or more items, the suffix *est* is often added

■ Realizing that an amount does not change in size even when placed in various containers of different sizes or shapes

Children practice logic, patterns, and counting skills as they determine and discuss measurement.

Children are using several different mathematical thinking skills as they are determining and discussing various measurements:

■ Logic and patterns as they identify length—long, short, tall; area—large, small; volume—full, empty, more, less; temperaturre—hot, cold, warm, cool; time—minute, hour, day; calendar—day, week, month, year; money—penny, nickel, dime, dollar; weight—heavy, light

■ Counting when describing the measurement of an item. (Since the standard measuring tools are too complex for children to use, you can have them use nonstandard items when they want to describe size—a book can be two feathers long and one feather wide.)

■ Logic when deciding which type of measuring tool is required

You can look around your room and find all sorts of tools and objects that will allow children to practice the various types of measurements possible. They need to have readiness experience with each type in order to begin to understand the limits of what each can measure. It is important to let children choose the types of containers and measuring tools and then, have them estimate (guess) about what will "fit."

REPORTING AND USING INFORMATION

Since children are already doing various types of abstract thinking, it is possible at an early age to introduce them to simple types of data reporting. Through their collecting and sorting of information for the reasoning activities, they are already gathering information that can be reported on a chart or graph. The graph just helps them organize the information so that a whole group can study the results and draw conclusions from the measurements or amounts shown.

Children will learn that comparing graphs is an easy way to compare groups of objects.

Graphs can be made of collections of real items first; then, a pictograph showing the same information can be constructed. Another step in this process would be to put up one example and then, let children make tally marks to stand for each one collecting that same example, Children can then make comparisons between the various columns or rows in the graph or chart and use terms such as "more than," "most, ""same," "least," "less than," and "none."

HIGHER-LEVEL THINKING

Higher-level thinking includes estimating, probability, and algebra.

This heading encompasses such abstract thinking mathematical areas as estimating, probability, and algebra. Yes, young children are already doing these types of thinking. They have been making guesses (estimating) a great deal during their measuring experiences and they should continue to do this in every one of the areas. Sampling one cookie to see if the batch is all right or deciding what the weather will be tomorrow are good examples of probability. Then, too, when children play spinner games, they will begin to see the probability of how often the arrow will land in a certain spot. And, last but not least, algebra does play a part in the young children's everyday lives. They do figure out different ways of sorting a group of objects into smaller groups. Children have been determining "unknowns" for a long time and, when they make one-to-one comparisons, they have been introduced to the concept of equality between certain sets and the inequality between others. (When children use a pan balance for instance, they are experimenting with these concepts.)

One area of higher-level thinking that should be stressed when working with young children is estimation because this allows children to bring into play so many of the other mathematical areas. This area is also important as children are attempting to solve problems.

CALCULATORS AND COMPUTERS

Young children are being exposed to calculators and computers at home and in school.

Much discussion is taking place right now about what mathematical and computational aids young children should be introduced to and when to introduce them. Since these aids are found both in homes and schools, you will find that perhaps many children in your classes are familiar with their appearances and some of their uses. In many cases, parents are allowing their children to manipulate the machines or sometimes youngsters are trying them out without guidance.

Therefore, we have included a few activities in *Counting on Math* where calculators and computers are discussed. Since the main advantage of a calculator is the speed by which computations can be made and that is not a goal with which young children should be concerned (They need to understand the operations that are possible on a calculator first.), your students can use the calculator as a place to read numbers and make them appear and disappear on the screen. With some children who understand about "moving groups together," and that numbers can stand for each of those groups, you may want to show them how that operation works on a calculator. Another skill that you should be teaching is the way to handle this rather delicate machine.

When introducing children to computers, the first item that should be discussed is the way to handle and care for this magic box. These complex machines can be easily affected by rough treatment, magnets, food spillage, incorrect usage and outside influences. Children will treat computers with respect if they are respectfully introduced to them and told what their limits and the machines' limits are. Young children should be introduced to the machine on an individual basis. You can, however, talk about the care of the machine with larger groups.

Computers can be used by children in two ways—first, playing games where they only have to press a few keys to operate or where they have to recognize the letters on the keyboard, and second, when they are able to use the computer as a word processor when writing stories. In either case, children have to be able to recognize what appears on the keyboard and understand that by pressing various keys certain functions can be performed.

Gauge the background and interests of your group and the capabilities of your facilities in deciding which of the calculator and computer activities you wish to introduce from this book.

PROBLEM SOLVING

An important aspect of mathematics is having its users be able to solve problems—both computational ones and other types. In many cases, people just make stabs at solutions without stopping to analyze the problem first and figure out that there may be more than one solution. Today, children are being encouraged to understand that some math problems have more than one correct answer so they need to figure out various solutions and that with other problems there is only one answer so they need to "learn" the appropriate number facts to answer those problems.

It is very important for children to learn the steps necessary to solve problems.

Most of the problems children meet have to be studied and the best way to solve the problem be considered. (The nice thing about problem solving is that it allows students to see that there is a purpose to what they have been studying.) Therefore, the youngsters need a plan for attempting to come up with a solution. Most elementary math programs teach problem-solving steps. Some steps that young children can apply are presented here.

1. Children have to recognize that there is a problem and that a solution is needed. (This is like "reading the problem.")
2. Children then have to talk about the problem so they know more about it—what is being asked, what information is there, what information is not there. (This is "knowing and thinking" about the problem.)
3. Children next need to plan what to do and make guesses about what will result if they make one choice over another. (They may need to make some trial runs and discover whether an idea will work.) (This is the "planning" and "choosing the operation" phase.)
4. Children should be allowed to try several strategies to see which idea will work best and then, to complete the activity that is supposed to solve their problem. (This is the "solving" the problem stage.)
5. It would be a good idea if children were able to talk about whether their solution worked out as they wanted it to, whether the answer obtained was reasonable, whether the next time they would solve it the same way or differently. (This is the "checking" and "evaluating" the solution step.)

You probably have been doing these steps all along, although you may not have put them together and shown children that it is a good idea to follow them in a set order. Pick a good situation, such as making plans for a special acitivity or day, and start out. It is always helpful when teachers and parents model the steps and processes that they want children to follow. You may even want to make some charts as you and the children go through the steps.

It will be fun to see when the children unconsciously begin to demonstrate the use of the steps. Here, again, you are not working for perfection. You are introducing and modeling processes which you hope they will begin to use so that they will become a natural part of their growth.

Dear Parents,

      This year, we will be encouraging your children to learn more about mathematics so they can use these skills on their own in their activities and discussion times. You can help at home by encouraging them to talk about activities they do at school and then, letting them apply the skills involved to situations at home.

      The areas being discussed are ones for which they already have the background. We are enlarging upon their knowledge so that they can continue to develop readiness for mathematics and to enable them to solve more problems on their own.

      These mathematical areas include :

Numbers—counting objects and learning the number
      system

Logic—classifying objects into various categories

Shapes—learning about geometric shapes and how
      they are used

Patterns—understanding and making different
      types of patterns

Measurement—discovering about measuring tools
      and what can be measured

Reporting and using information—making and
      using simple graphs and charts

Higher-level thinking—using more abstract
      thinking when guessing, figuring out probabilities,
      and thinking about unknowns

    Come to school and see the type of work your children are doing and we can discuss ways that you can continue to enhance their knowledge of mathematics. Remember that your children will have to count on their mathematical knowledge for many years to come!

    We just want to give each and every child a good boost on the way up!

                  Your child's teacher

ALL
ABOUT
ME

ALL ABOUT ME

Number
Mirror, Mirror on the Wall

Children become aware of the "numberness" of things in their lives at a very early age even though they do not know the words that indicate what amounts are being talked about or used. They see, for instance, their two hands or five fingers. Now, when they are older and are discussing their own individuality, it would be helpful again to let them indicate "how many" or "amounts" in concrete ways. By using a mirror, they can "see" the amounts. Let children point to each item in turn. If children know number words, encourage their use as in COUNT ON ME.

Place a large mirror in the room. You may also want to have small mirrors nearby. Let children take turns using a mirror. Name different body parts and ask children to point to each one. Let them discuss the "amounts" of noses and mouths versus the "amounts" of eyes, ears, arms, or legs in any numerical terminology they wish. Other body parts you may want to include are as follows: "one"—head, chin, stomach; "two"—hands, knees, feet. Make this a time of discovery so that children may also realize the similarity in the number of fingers on each hand or that the number of toes on one foot equals the number of fingers on one hand.

Reasoning
What Are We Like?

As children are discussing body parts, they will probably sense that most of them have the same number of each kind. They may begin also to realize that there are differences too—hair coloring, height, color of eyes, weight, and so on. It will help children in developing reasoning skills to realize that "things" can be grouped by these differences.

Start the game by picking a category that enables some children to become part of a specific group, such as those with red hair. Ask those children to stand together so that the whole group can see the similarity. Ask the group to name another hair color and to find the members of that category. Continue this until each child is in a specific group. Right away, come up with a different category—such as the color of shoes. Let children think up other categories in which to divide themselves—sex, height, types of clothing—and form those groups.

Shapes
The Shape of the World

As children look about their environments, they are visualizing two- and three- dimensional shapes. They sense the differences and, through their experimentation with actual objects, understand more about the shapes. Through feeling objects, they can build shape pictures in their minds.

Have children look at things on their clothing that have simple shape descriptors, such as buttons and patterns and designs in fabric. (Manufacturers of children's clothing often decorate them with simple shapes.) Let them see a shape in the mirror and rub a finger around it. Then, display both two- and three-dimensional examples of circular and rectangular shaped objects so children can trace around their edges.

COUNT ON ME

YOU'LL NEED:

Chair

counting rhyme

"One, Two, I see you.
Three, four, here are more.
Five, six, hands do tricks.
Seven, eight, stop, let's wait.
Nine, ten, start again."

WHAT TO DO:

 1. Have children say the counting rhyme along with you and do the actions as suggested.

 2. "ONE, TWO, I See YOU."

Have child put both hands over both eyes as if sighting something far away.

 3. "THREE, FOUR, Here are more."

Have child stretch out both legs and point to them.

 **4.** "FIVE, SIX, Hands do tricks."

Have child clap hands and then intertwine fingers on both hands.

 5. "Seven, eight, Stop, let's wait."

Have child put up hand in a 'stop' motion.

 6. "Nine, ten, start again."

Have child roll both arms around each other.

ALL ABOUT ME

Patterns
What Comes Next?

In order to solve problems in mathematics, children need to be able to organize the information given, whether it be in pictures, numerals, or words. It is helpful when they can see patterns among the data. The search for patterns begins with concrete objects. Usually children first are asked to add parts to existing patterns. They study what is already there and then they decide what comes next. They realize that in a pattern there is more than one object and there has to be at least one difference between the objects before the pattern is repeated. In order to understand patterns, children must first be able to figure out the differences and then sort the objects into their groups as is shown in PRINT AND SORT. After some practice with continuing patterns, they then can create their own.

Draw a left shoeprint on a sheet of construction paper and a right print on the same color paper. Make copies and let children cut out either a right or a left one. Have them name which shoeprint they have or show which one it is by matching it to their correct foot. Start the pattern by helping a child put down a left print and stand with that foot forward. Help another child put down a right shoeprint and step forward on that foot. Continue aiding children to build more of the pattern in the same way several more times. Then, let them choose which print "comes next." (If children are familiar with patterns, make each type of footprint using two different colors of construction paper and follow the same procedure, using two variables: red/right—blue/left—red/left—blue/right.)

Measurement
Find Out About Fit

Because objects in the children's world have "shapes," they also have dimensions and can be measured in different ways. Our language contains labels for these measurements and they can be used when comparing objects.

Have different pairs of children stand next to each other so the group can see the differences in height. Be sure to have a shorter child become a taller one by changing the person with whom the comparison is made. Children can also compare differences in the size of their hands or feet. Let children measure and describe the size of objects in the room according to different parts of their bodies, such as, "*That bug is the same size as the fingernail on my little finger,* or," *my foot fits on top of this block.*"

Let children draw around a foot and cut out the pattern. Put two pieces of masking tape on the floor four feet apart. Have various children place their prints across to show how many "feet" apart the tapes are.

PRINT and SORT

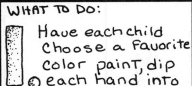

YOU'LL NEED:

6" square cards (four for each child)   paints   5 styrofoam trays lined with paper towels (to hold each paint color)

WHAT TO DO:

1 Have each child choose a favorite color paint, dip each hand into it and print the left hand on one card and the right hand on another.

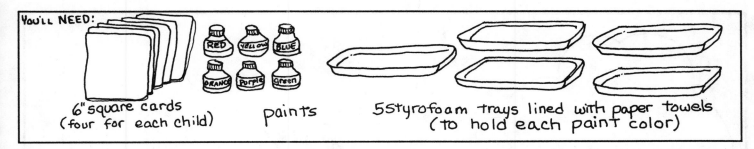

2 Have each child choose a favorite color paint, dip each foot into it and print left foot on one card and right foot on another.

3 Have children sort cards in following ways:
- ☆ all right hands
- ☆ all left hands
- ☆ all right feet
- ☆ all left feet
- ☆ all red prints

...and so on. Save cards for future games.

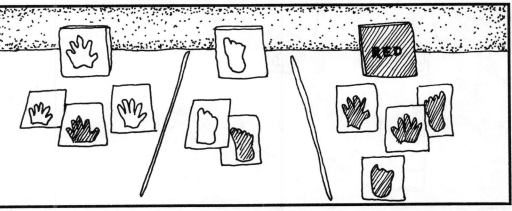

SHAPING A SCENE

Connect the things that are alike to make: a ——line, a ☐ , a △ and a
☆ or a ⬠ or a ⊙. Circle everything else that is alone. Color the picture.

33

DISCOVERY TIME

As children work or play in everyday situations, they need to encounter problems that require them to experience and practice various math concepts. In developing areas of the room, be sure to display objects that will encourage experimentation and attempts to solve problems.

One such area is the HOUSEKEEPING CORNER. In it, you will probably want to include items such as the following:

- tables and chairs
- dolls and stuffed animals
- dishes
- dress-up clothing
- empty containers
- measuring cups
- toy telephone

- stove
- pots and pans
- plastic flatware
- doll clothes
- plastic glassware
- play tools

At the beginning, just observe as children use some of the above props. See what problems occur and how each is solved. After there has been some time for children to discover solutions on their own, you may wish to pose problems that cover parts of major math skill areas not yet explored, such as some of those given below.

NUMBER

- How many children can play in the housekeeping corner?
- Are there enough cups for everyone?
- How will you divide that pie you have baked?
- How will you pass out the milk?

REASONING

- What kind of food will the dolls eat?
- What type of dish belongs on that shelf?
- Will all or some of the doll clothes fit that doll?

SHAPES

- Where will you put these plates?
- How can you put these boxes away so we will have more room?

PATTERNS

- How do you place the spoons and forks when setting a table?
- When it's time to put the dolls away, what order will you use as you place them on the shelf?

MEASUREMENT

- Which doll fits best into that bed?
- Find the shoes that go together so you can dress the doll.
- How much water will you need to make oatmeal?
- Which measuring tools will we use when making bread?

RECORDING AND USING INFORMATION

- How can we show what are the favorite foods of the children in this class?
- How will we decide what kind of bread to make?

LANGUAGE DEVELOPMENT

LANGUAGE DEVELOPMENT

Number
Eeney, Meeney, Miney, Mo

When children begin to discover mathematical concepts, they have not yet developed a wide vocabulary. You can help increase the young people's knowledge by providing terms. Be sure to consistently use and demonstrate the same wording or show what is meant by a new term.

As children pass out brushes or snacks, let them count. Grab a small group of paintbrushes (no more than five) and say, *"Let's find out 'how many' we have."* Have children help count as you hold up each one. When you and the children say the last number, point out that the last number word said tells "how many" there were. Show some of the brushes, and then, send children to find that same number of books, crayons, or dolls. As each child returns with objects, let the group count the objects as the "finder" points to them.

Shapes
What's My Shape?

Each geometric shape has a fancy name and children love to learn words like "circle," "square," "triangle," and "rectangle." Adults also use synonyms or descriptive terms when talking about these shapes. Children need to be made aware of all the definitions and the various shades of meaning.

Group children around the block corner or a set of three-dimensional shapes that includes a circle (sphere), square (cube), rectangle (block), and triangle (cone). Hold up any one of the shapes and let children name or describe what they see, using whatever words they know. You may want to have them name other items that are shaped the same way. Present each child with a two-dimensional, paper version of one of the shapes discussed or let them use the ones made in SEW A SHAPE. Let each child find an example of the shape she or he has and place the paper shape on the example and describe what they found.

Reasoning
What Do You Think?

As children develop their language abilities, they are better able to explain how they solve problems and adults can provide better guidance. Children will benefit from having a good understanding of and using terms such as the following: "all," "some," "none," "every," "many," "few," "alike," "same," "different," "group," "go together."

Sorting sets of different shapes that come in several colors requires children to use their reasoning abilities. Use attribute blocks or something similar. Point to one shape and ask children to find all the other blocks that are shaped the same way. Next, have them find some of those blocks that are blue. Each time, ask children to describe what they are doing. Then, at a later time, ask them to show how they would sort all the blocks into groups of shapes that are alike.

SEW A SHAPE

YOU'LL NEED:

styrofoam meat trays   yarn   pencil   tape   yarn needle   scissors

WHAT TO DO:

1. Use a sharp pencil point to poke holes into styrofoam tray in a geometric shape. Make sure to poke an even number of holes.

2. Prepare yarn by cutting an 18" length and tightly taping one end almost into a point. Knot the other end. Or, use a yarn needle and yarn.

3. Have children sew the shape outline on tray by putting the yarn through each hole. Knot to finish.

LANGUAGE DEVELOPMENT

Patterns
Follow the Leaders

When children are continuing or making patterns, they are using many of the same skills and the same terms that are a part of reasoning. In addition, they have to think about the "order words" that help explain the way a pattern appears and grows—what is first, what comes next, what follows after, and so on. (Shapes and pattern-making go hand in hand.)

Use a set of small, different-shaped, two-dimensional blocks that has at least three or four different colors in it. Make patterns using two different shapes that are the same color, such as the following: red square—red circle—red square—red circle—red square. Have children make the same pattern right below the one you made. The next time, make similar patterns and ask them to tell and to show what shape comes after the last one you put down. Children will do the same type of activity in MYSTERY PATTERNS. Encourage them to name the items in the complete pattern using order words. When possible, make the patterns harder by using different shapes and colors. (If you have different sized blocks, children later on can make patterns by arranging shapes in order by size.)

Measurement
What Can You Say About Me?

Young children sense that objects have some type of dimensions. They know, for instance, when the milk bottle is full and when it is empty. They realize that objects have size or amount variations, that there are differences in weight, and that differing amounts can be put into containers. As children grow older, "measurement" words pop up in their conversations because they hear adults using them. Be sure to help children realize what each word means by presenting concrete examples. You also need to show that sometimes the words used depend upon what is being compared. (A taller person may become the shorter one if that person stands next to someone who has grown more.)

Introduce size words—"small," "short," "big," "tall," "wide," "narrow," "skinny," "long," "whole," "half"—by first letting children compare two objects, such as two chairs. Have children point to the bigger one or the smaller one. They may also want to describe them as the taller chair or the shorter chair. Let one child pick up each chair and then tell which one is heavier and which is lighter. Another time, use different sized pots and pans. Have children first describe them using size words. Next, give them opportunities to fill some of the biggest pans and then use that water to fill other smaller containers. Ask children to describe what is happening. (This would be a good time for them to discover which pan is heavier and which is lighter when a pan is full or empty.)

Let children count out two groups of differing amounts of counters and decide which one has more or which one has less (or fewer) items in it.

MYSTERY PATTERNS

YOU'LL NEED:

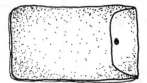
a 10" x 13" manilla envelope

markers

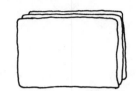
8½" x 11" pieces of paper

stickers

WHAT TO DO:

1. Prepare mystery envelope by labelling it and adding a large question mark. Draw outline of a door on flap.

2. Prepare patterns by adhering stickers in simple patterns onto the horizontal midline of each sheet of paper. Place sheets in envelope.

3. Open the 'door' and slowly pull out one pattern sheet. Say the following sequence: "First, the heart, the pumpkin is second, the boat is third." Pull out the next symbol (heart) and ask children, "What comes next?"

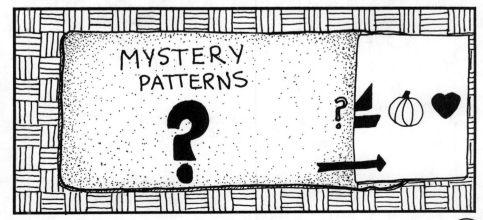

CIRCUS

Help the ringmaster place each type of animal into the best circus train car.

TRAIN

Draw a line from the animals to the best car.

DISCOVERY TIME

You can provide materials for math activities in each of your special corners—dramatic play, water table, blocks, science, art, library—as you will see in the forthcoming units. By also setting up a separate MATH CENTER, you can provide opportunities for this type of learning to take place in a more organized environment. (Some materials for each major area of a math program are suggested below.) In any case, be sure that children have a chance to experiment with the materials and try to solve problems.

NUMBER (*"How Many?"*)

■ Objects to count, such as buttons, beads, dishes, silverware
■ Objects such as those above that can be added to, taken away from, multiplied, or divided
■ Objects that have numbers on them, such as a telephone, clock, calendar, calculator
■ Number cards with and without amounts shown

REASONING (*"Where do these belong?"*)

■ Similar objects that are different colors, sizes, shapes, or kinds that can be sorted into "sets" or "groups," such as foods, blocks
■ Objects to count—such as buttons, beads, dishes, silverware, blocks—sort into groups, and describe as "all," "some," "none"
■ Containers into which items can be sorted, such as cans, dishes

SHAPES (*"What do I look like?" or "What's my name?"*)

■ Examples of three-dimensional shapes—balls, globes, blocks
■ Examples of two-dimensional shapes—clocks, plates; drawing paper
■ Sets of attribute blocks
■ Waistband elastic or rubber bands
■ Geoboards

PATTERNS (*"What comes next?"*)

■ Sets of beads and string
■ Pegs and pegboards
■ Sets of attribute blocks

MEASUREMENT (*"What's its size?" "What will fit?"*)

■ Containers of all different sizes and shapes
■ Objects of all different sizes and shapes
■ measuring devices—cups, spoons, rulers, balance, scale
■ Clocks—regular and digital

REPORTING AND USING INFORMATION (*"How will we show what we found out?"*)

■ Calendars
■ Weather charts
■ Paper for making graphs or charts

MATHEMATICAL AIDS (*"Will this make your work easier?"*)

■ Calculator
■ Abacus
■ Computer
■ Counters

SEASONS

FALL

Number
How Many Days 'til Fall?

One way of introducing the use of written numbers is through a calendar. Here children can see the usual order in which numbers appear in a real-life situation. It is hard, however, for them to understand the passage of time and how that is counted. By using the calendar and talking about events that occur daily, children can begin to sense "time lengths" as they are learning to read numbers.

Help children develop a system for "counting down" until fall arrives "by the calendar" or until lots of fall signs appear. For instance, use a portion of each box on the calendar to indicate weather signs that occur daily. Discuss with children what some of the fall signs are (leaves changing color, weather turning more brisk, flowers dying, animals searching for and storing food, and so on). Let children take turns drawing a picture of any sign that happens on that date on the calendar. When the fall signs seem to appear frequently, help children count to see how many days have passed since they began marking the calendar.

Reasoning
Bringing Groups Back

Fall is a good time to go collecting, and collections mean that you and the children have to think about how to group what has been brought back. Let them use their reasoning skills to devise different ways of sorting what they find.

Take a walk around the neighborhood with the children and let them pick up samples of different objects that they find. (You may want to suggest that they include only signs of fall or you may wish to let children expand their treasure hunt to all types of small things that children can carry.) Provide each child with a paper or plastic bag in which their finds can be kept and then, let the group hunt. After the search is over, let children sort what they have found by telling them to group together things that are alike in some way. If they need help deciding upon ways of grouping, show two items that are similar except for one difference—two differently colored leaves; one rough piece of tree bark, one smoother type; one leaf with smooth edges, one with rough edges.

Measurement
How Long Is That Time?

In order for children to understand the passage of long periods of time, they first need to have a feel for short time spans. Children will begin to grasp "time terms" if they can relate events to the length of time being discussed.

Point to the time on a clock and let children get dressed in their fall outer garments and then see how many "minutes" it takes for them to put on sweaters, jackets, and caps. Help children "see" the passage of a day by discussing how the sun seems to move across the sky during a day and how that movement affects the size of the shadows that are cast. Use SHADOW MEASURING to help children explore time passage and body length.

SHADOW MEASURING

YOU'LL NEED:

roll of paper

marker   clock

sunny day

WHAT TO DO:

1. Help child place strips of paper on a sidewalk or driveway. Paper should be placed approximately East/West so that it will catch child's shadow. Hold down with rocks.

2. On a sunny day, at about 9:00 a.m., have child stand very still at the bottom of paper so that whole shadow fits on paper.

3. Have another child or another adult trace outline of the shadow as it falls on the paper.

4. At 12:00 noon — the same day — reposition the child (and paper if necessary) so that child's shadow again falls onto paper.

5. Have another child or another adult trace the outline of shadow as it now falls onto paper.

6. Compare, with children, each of their two outlines. What happened? Why? What do children think the shadows would look like later in the afternoon?

FALL

Shapes
What Shapes Are Here?

One type of sorting that children can easily do is by the shape of objects. During the fall, they will see both two- and three-dimensional items; they may also find objects that are made up of parts of different shapes—the rounded edges of a flat maple leaf, the roundness of an apple with its somewhat heart-shaped portion where it had been attached to a tree.

From the science corner or on one of the fall walks, let children collect items that are two-dimensional, such as leaves. Have them place a sheet of paper over one of the objects and move the side of a crayon over the paper. Ask children to describe what shapes they see in each rubbing. (You can also give children the outlines of leaf shapes and let them try to find leaves outside that match each shape.)

Patterns
Making Natural Necklaces

Children like to see and make patterns, and there are many things that are harvested in the fall that can be used to make "orderly" designs—kernels of corn, leaves, seeds, pumpkins, fruits, vegetables, and nuts.

After children have bought or harvested a pumpkin, help them separate out the seeds. Bring in also different types of beans that have been dried. Let each child pick out some pumpkin seeds and one kind of bean. Provide each child with a blunt-ended needle and some thin wire. Let each one design a pattern for a necklace and string the elements on the wire. Help children fasten the end of their necklaces.

Reporting and Using Information
How Many Did We Find?

A pictograph is the simplest way of graphing information because it shows more concrete examples of what is being counted and displayed.

Make a very realistic pictograph by using actual objects. Put an example of each kind of seed that could be found on a "seed walk" on the left side of a sheet of paper and draw horizontal lines to separate the kinds. Let children hunt for seeds and pin their finds in the proper sections. Help the group count the number of each kind of seeds and then write the total at the right edge. Children can also graph the shapes of leaves using KINDS OF LEAVES.

Buy or collect some different types of apples. Let each child study an apple. Using paper and glue, help children make a realistic pictograph, using the apples or drawings of them, by picking one category—size, variety, weight, number of seeds inside—and figuring out what the column headings would be. Let each child place her or his apple in the appropriate column.

KINDS OF LEAVES

You'll Need:

posterboard

marker

leaves

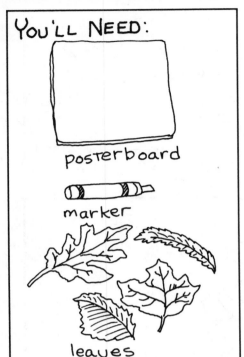

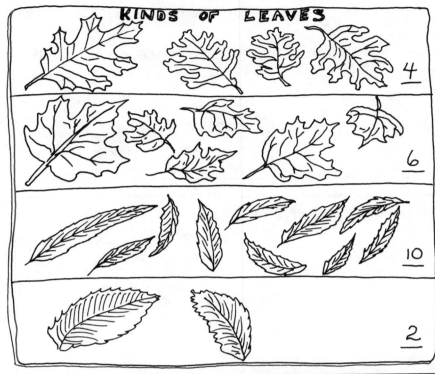

KINDS OF LEAVES

4

6

10

2

What To Do:

1. Make a graph by placing one example of 3 or 4 different leaves along the left side, down in a column, of a large piece of posterboard.

2. Then draw horizontal lines to separate each type of leaf.

3. Have children hunt for these leaves outside. Each leaf is then placed on space on chart that matches its geometric shape.

4. Have children count the number of each type of leaf.

5. Have children record the total number of each type of leaf at the right side on the blank line.

6. Discuss, with children, the number of leaves - which types have more?, less?, the same number?

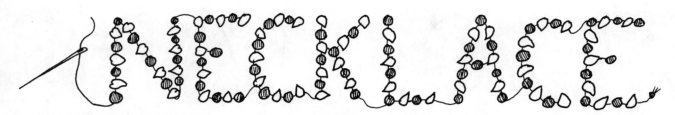

NECKLACE

You'll Need To Do:

First, have children finish the pattern on this page and color it in as desired.

Then, have children make a real necklace with seeds and beans.

pumpkin seeds   beans   needle   thread   warm water

(black)

(northern)

(soak beans and seeds for ½ hour.)

FINISH THE NECKLACE BY ADDING THE SEEDS AND BEANS.
COLOR THE NECKLACE.

FALL

DISCOVERY TIME

Children will enjoy using their mathematical knowledge as they watch the seasons pass. Provide them with many opportunities to use different types of concrete materials as they are working out any mathematical problems that occur during their play or as they think about science and social studies projects. Below are some concrete materials and their major areas for development.

NUMBER

Use the following objects as counters. Use the calendar so that children can begin to read numbers, as well as learning to count the days in a week and in a month.

- Leaves
- Acorns
- Flowers
- Ears of corn
- Rocks
- Gourds
- Twigs
- Seeds
- Pumpkins
- Feathers
- Nuts
- Horse chestnuts

REASONING

Use these objects to sort by size, shape, color, texture, living or non-living, edible or non-edible, and by function.

- Leaves
- Flowers
- Seed pods
- Seeds
- Stones
- Bark
- Nuts
- Feathers
- Gourds
- Cones
- Vegetables
- Pebbles

MEASUREMENT

Use objects as standard and non-standard measurement for time, length, temperature, and weight.

- Clock
- Boxes
- String
- Magnifying glass
- Balance
- Feathers
- Paper chain
- Calendar
- Sundial
- Timer
- Baskets
- Thermometer

SHAPES

Use these natural examples of three-dimensional objects to encourage descriptions and comparisons.

- Apples
- Gourds
- Nuts
- Pebbles
- Pumpkins
- Seed pods

PATTERNS

Use the objects to help children discover patterns in nature. Also have children copy and/or extend basic patterns.

- Seeds
- Pine needles
- Leaves
- Fruits and vegetables
- Gourds

REPORTING AND USING INFORMATION

Use these objects directly on charts and graphs.

- Seeds
- Feathers
- Insects
- Pine needles
- Fruits
- Twigs
- Leaves
- Cones
- Vegetables

WINTER

Number
What's the Order?

While children are "learning" to count, they begin to realize that the numbers are usually said in a certain order. At the same time, they are hearing other words that have to do with order such as "first," "second," "third;" "first," "next," "last"; "before," "after." It would be helpful to indicate which object you are talking about whenever you use one or more of these words. You must also indicate one other aspect each time you refer to order—your starting point, usually the left side if you are going in a horizontal direction. Remember also to face the same way as the children are looking when you discuss left and right. Be consistent, too, when deciding which is your starting point as you talk about vertical direction.

Discuss with children the steps to be followed in making a snowman. You may want to begin simply by having them roll three snowballs of varying sizes. Ask children to count the snowballs while they are all still on the ground; then indicate each by the order word you wish to use. Have them tell by the correct order word how each is to be placed to make a snowman. Then, discuss the order in which the snow statue will be completed— body parts, clothing, and so on.

Estimating
How many Handfuls?

Working with snow, water, mud, or sand gives children many opportunities to estimate, or guess, amounts. When they do this, as in MELTING RACE, they are using mental arithmetic.

Sometimes when children are building something small, ask different ones to tell how many handfuls of material they think they will need. Keep track of the guesses and then the actuality and discuss the amounts with the children.

Children can help develop patterns by making "designs" on different types of materials. These designs may include using various shapes, sizes, and colors.

Bring out pieces of burlap and let children cut out mitten shapes for either one or both hands—they can cut them freehand or by first tracing around a hand or a mitten pattern. Give children lengths of yarn, one end of each having been covered with clear tape to form a needle and the other end being knotted. Let them weave in and out of the burlap and make up their own designs. Some may want to use only one color; others more than one. (Children may want to make both mittens match; you can attach them with a long string so children can keep track of the two they made.

Also have some plain mittens set aside. Hang up a clothesline and let children develop some type of orderly pattern—left hand/ right hand, one plain/one with a design, and so on.

MELTING RACE

WHOSE	WHERE	ORDER OF MELTING
Annie	Refrigerator	7
Jen	wrapped in newspaper	6
Kate	radiator	1
Hillary	shelf	2
Scott	window sill	5
Sarah	play refrig.	2
Frankie	front hall	4
Seth	sink	3

ORANGE JUICE — Kate

ORANGE JUICE — Annie

ORANGE JUICE — Hillary

ORANGE JUICE — Sarah

FASTEST MELTING   SLOWEST MELTING   MELTED AT THE SAME TIME

YOU'LL NEED:

one orange juice can per child

snow or crushed ice

paper

markers

WHAT TO DO:

1. Have children collect snow out-of-doors and pack it into orange juice cans.

2. Have children choose and then place their filled cans anywhere inside the classroom.

3. Observe the snow in the cans. Determine which can's snow melts fastest, slowest, and so on. Discuss and then record the relationship between rate of melting and place where can was put.

WINTER

Reasoning
Who Has Been Here?

As children play outside in the winter, they can become detectives using "footprint" clues in the snow (or mud or sand) to find out who (or what) has been there before them. First, help them sort these clues by the "large" group to which each belong—animals, persons, transportation (things with wheels), tools, and so on. Then, see if they can divide each general category into the members that might belong to it—dogs, bicycle, snow shovel. Have children explain how they made their decisions.

After a snowstorm or rain, take children on a walk outside. Let them make tracks in some clean snow, a smooth muddy area, or sand and then examine the shapes. Next, explain that they are detectives looking for clues to see who or what else has been outside nearby. Compliment children as they use terms like "animal tracks" or "paw marks," bird's feet, "where a cat sat," or "tire tracks." Let those, who are able, tell, for instance, what specific animal made a certain track or what vehicle made a specific type of tire track.

Measurement
How Often Did It Snow?

Measurement also involves keeping records of amounts—how often does some weather phenomena occur, and, when they do, how much rain or snow comes down, for instance. Help children understand that a weather calendar, thermometer, and some type of rain gauge can be measuring tools.

On the main classroom calendar or on a separate one, help children keep track of the types of weather that occur during a certain month. At the end of each time period, show them how to count up and record somewhere how many days of each type they experienced. If you use a symbol like a mitten to indicate "very cold" days, you may want, at the same time, to introduce the use of a thermometer and show how it records different temperatures. Each day, one temperature reading can be recorded on a mitten.

Higher-Level Thinking
How many Ways?

It will be helpful to children in later life if they have experiences in their early years that prepare them for the abstract thinking. Pre-algebraic activities, such as SNOWBALL COUNTERS and the one below, can easily be fit into Early Childhood lesson plans.

Bring the pan balance outside and then, have children form different-sized snowballs or make ice cubes of varying sizes. Have them experiment with placing items on each side so that the balance shows that the sides are even in weight. Help them count the objects on each side.

SNOWBALL COUNTERS

10 large styrofoam balls

marker

2 large pickle-type jars (available from restaurants)

posterboard

10 SNOWBALLS

4 and 6

2 and 8

5 and

9 and 1

3 and 7

WHAT TO DO:

1. Have children count out ten styrofoam balls.

2. Have children place all ten balls into either of the two jars in any combination:

4 and 6	10 and 0
3 and 7	9 and 1
8 and 2	5 and 5

3. Help children make a chart showing the combinations. Use pictures and stress the many ways and combinations that make the number ten.

FROSTY SHAPES

YOU'LL NEED:

epsom salts

water

measuring cup

bowl

brushes

crayons

colored paper

white paper

scissors

WHAT TO DO:

1. Cut colored Construction paper into several sizes and shapes of the basic ○, □, ▭ and △.

2. Encourage children to use these cut-out shapes, with glue, to make winter scenes on a background piece of dark construction paper.

3. Have children use crayons to add details to their work.

4. Mix a Solution of one cup of epsom salts and $\frac{1}{2}$ cup water. Mix well.

5. Have children 'paint' solution with brushes over entire picture. Dry Thoroughly. Lovely crystals will form over the picture like 'frost'.

6. Cut out window pane squares from white paper and glue it onto each window—winter scene picture.

WINTER

DISCOVERY TIME

Winter is an excellent time to apply mathematical skills both inside and out because weather patterns tend to be so variable. Mathematics can be applied in many activities that take place before, during, and after a change in the weather. Included in the following are some materials that you may want to have on hand.

NUMBER

Use these items to count as well a develop one-to-one correspondence and the idea of ordinal numbers.
- Snowsuits
- Caps
- Shovels
- Boots
- Mittens
- Cotton balls

REASONING

Use these categories to have children determine what belongs in each category.
- Clothing
- Tools
- Footwear
- Animals
- Food
- Things that go
- Jobs
- Shelter
- Foul weather gear

SHAPES

These are examples of various three-dimensional shapes. Each can be used to discuss the basic shape of the item and function.
- Boxes
- Skis and poles
- Ice skates
- Hats
- Shovels
- Icicles
- Scarves
- Sleds
- Boots
- Mittens

ESTIMATING

Use these materials to have children practice making estimations.
- Calendar
- Thermometer
- Ice maker

MEASUREMENT

Use these objects to discuss how different tools are used. Discuss not only what each tool measures, but how it does so, and what is recorded.
- Calendar
- Rain
- Scale
- Weather chart
- Hot water
- Balance
- Gauge
- Ice cubes
- Weather symbols
- Rulers
- Containers
- Thermometer
- Magnifying glass

HIGHER-LEVEL THINKING

Discuss how these items can be used by children to make up their own problems and their own solutions to these problems.
- Balance
- Cotton balls
- Jars
- Dough
- Clay
- Ice cubes

SPRING

Number
How Many in All?

Children continually do adding and subtracting. For several reasons, they don't realize what "operation" is taking place but they still can figure out the right answers. One reason is that we don't tell them each time what "big operation" they are doing. Then, too, we quite frequently use different words to mean the same type of operation: addition—"how many in all," "how many altogether," "add," "join," "count up," "include," "put with"; subtraction— "take away," "move away," "how many less." It helps young children to understand what is being done if we are consistent in terminology and they can visualize the operations and move objects apart and together. They need to work with concrete examples before they can be expected to use abstract thinking.

Take a spring walk and have children look for objects that first can be counted and then, that can be grouped in some way. For instance, have them find out how many flowers there are in one flower bed. (Pick a bed that has only one or two flowers.) If children have permission, let them pick the flowers and take the bunch over to another bed that has only two or three flowers in it. Help them count and pick the ones in the new bed. Then, back in the room, have children find out how many flowers there are "in all" so that the right number of bud vases can be found. Remind children how many there were in each group. Ask them to tell how many all together.

You can also use SAND CASTING to provide them another opportunity for counting and adding.

Reasoning
Who's in the Family?

During the spring season, it is a good time to talk about sorting "family" groups. At this time of the year, mother animals and their new babies do not always resemble each other so the sorting job is a little harder.

Use pictures, drawings, plastic replicas, stuffed animals, or live animals for display purposes. Let children talk about the similarities and differences between each adult animal and its young. Separate animals by age groups and then, let children match families.

Shapes
Where Are the Shapes?

Children enjoy looking for shapes in everyday life. This is helpful, too, because then they can see the importance of that shape and "how" it is used.

Introduce and talk about new shapes that have not been discussed very much so far. Inside the room, one of those shapes that will be appearing is the oval or egg shape. Provide dyes so that children can decorate their eggs. This will provide them opportunities to "feel" the contours of an oval.

Outside, show children a baseball field and let them walk all the way around the bases starting from home plate. Draw a picture of what the field looks like on a piece of paper or a board. Let children see if they can find other examples of the diamond shape—some highway signs, for instance.

SAND CASTING

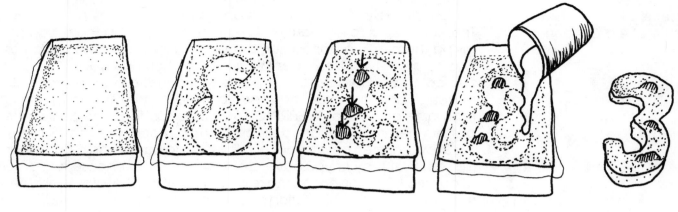

WHAT TO DO:

1. Have children line the shoe box with plastic wrap and place moist sand 3/4's of the way up the inside of the box.

2. Have children use their hands or a block to make a large depression in the sand in the form of a number. Remember to reverse most numbers! (NOT 1, 0, or 8.)

3. Have children choose stones — one for the number one casting, two for the number two, three for the number three and so on.

4. Have children place the stone(s) into the number impression. Have children push the stone(s) slightly deeper into the impression so they are partially buried.

5. Mix Plaster of Paris according to directions and immediately pour it into number impression. Let set 1/2 to one hour.

6. Pry the number up out of the sand. Brush off excess sand. Make a whole set of these number sculptures with their stone counters!

SPRING

Patterns
Let's Make a Garden

Children, by now, have seen and continued many patterns. The next step is to let them make up their own. Help them start by giving them only a limited number of variations to include, such as two colors or two sizes. Then, widen their choices: three colors or two colors and two sizes. Remind children that a pattern "repeats" its design after the order has been decided. They are using their reasoning powers, as in SPRING TALLIES, to sort the members of the pattern before they start to place them in order.

Show children how to make tulips by tracing around a cardboard pattern that they or you have created. Let them choose two colors of construction paper and make a number of tulip blooms. Help them make thin green construction paper "stems" and then, provide them with a sheet of newsprint or other white paper. Let children choose three of their tulip tops, decide what type of pattern will be used in "planting" a garden—changing color every other time; having one of one color and two of the other; having two of one color and one of the other—and paste down the beginning of the pattern. Have them repeat the pattern.

Measurement
How Does Your Garden Grow?

Measurement often means a continuing process when people deal with objects that grow. Spring is a good time of year to discuss this because growth changes can be shown more graphically. Children can use rulers or nonstandard measures to indicate the growth patterns of plants, animals, and incomplete buildings.

Provide each child with cutoff plastic milk cartons or paper cups, some soil, and several examples of two different types of seeds. Let children plant each kind of seed in one of the containers. Help them keep track of how long it takes each type to sprout. After the first green appears, have children place a tongue depressor by each seedling. Help them mark the height of each sprout on its depressor each day to see how high and how fast each one grows.

When people decide that they are going to plant a garden, they have to do a lot of planning before they ever start. There are lots of numerical decisions to make—how big the garden will be, how many rows to make, what will be planted in each row, how many seeds will be placed in each row, how many tomato plants will provide the amount of tomatoes a family wants that year.

Higher-Level Thinking
Let's Plan a Garden

Help children plan a garden, using either a plot outside or the sandbox area or water table. Pose some of the problems suggested above and let children discuss decisions and their reasons for making certain abstract ones. You will need to help children read the planting suggestions given on packets of seeds. Let them decide how a certain number of tomato plants or other seedlings or starts can be placed in a garden—all in one row or in two or three rows—and explain their answers. Have them think about their answers before they actually place the plants in position.

SPRING TALLIES

BLOSSOMS

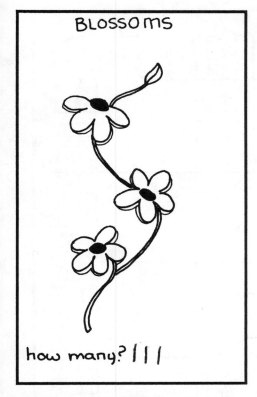

how many? | | |

BIRDS

how many? | |

PLANTS SPROUTING

how many? | |

INSECTS

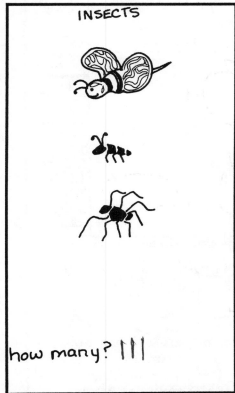

how many? | | |

PLACES WHERE SNOW IS MELTING

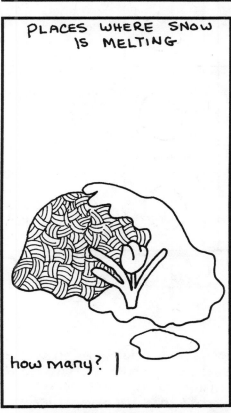

how many? |

BABY ANIMALS

how many? | |

Have children take these cards with them on a spring walk. Have children make tally marks on each card as they see the item. Example: | | | | | . (Reproduce sheet and cut each card apart, if desired.)

PLANTING A GARDEN

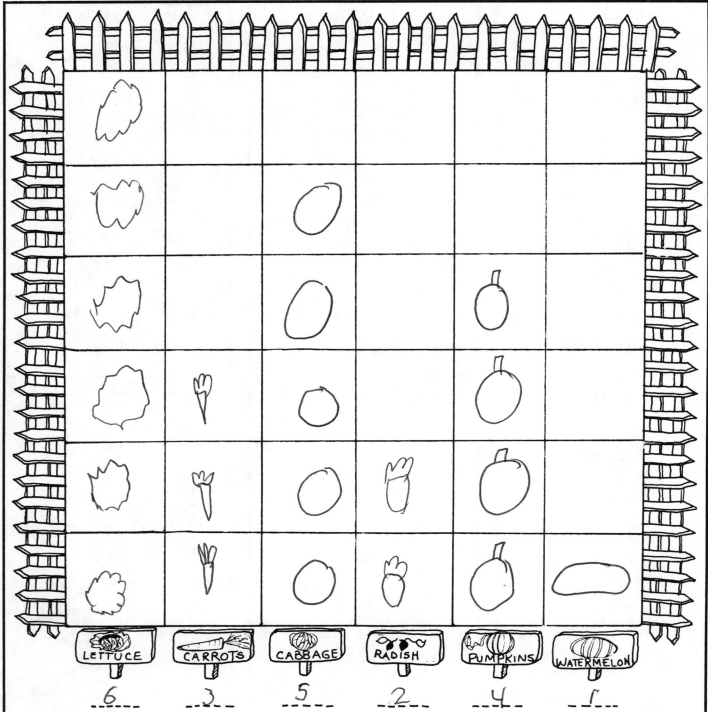

LETTUCE	CARROTS	CABBAGE	RADISH	PUMPKINS	WATERMELON
6	3	5	2	4	1

WHAT to Do: Write a number from 1 to 6 on each of the blanks at bottom of each column. Have child draw in or glue on that number of tissue paper plants up and down in that column. To make tissue paper plants: Each head of lettuce is a green ball; carrots are orange pieces of rolled paper; cabbage is purple; radishes are small red balls; pumpkins are orange balls and watermelons are large green balls!

DISCOVERY TIME

Many springtime mathematical challenges occur outside. You should prepare your room since April showers may prevent outdoor walks or gardening. Here are suggestions of materials or places that may be available.

NUMBER

Use the following objects as counters and as objects that can be added to, subtracted from, multiplied , and divided.

- Seeds
- Garden tools
- Flowers
- Nests
- Plants
- Seedlings
- Eggs
- Leaves

REASONING

Use these objects to sort by size, shape, color, texture, living or non-living, and by function.

- Seeds
- Toy farms
- Flowers
- Tools
- Birds
- Plants
- Toy workers
- Shelters
- Nests
- Leaves
- Animals
- Foods

SHAPES

These are examples of three dimensional shapes that can be used for encourging descriptions and as a basis for comparisons.

- Eggs
- Playing fields
- Spades
- Pails
- Leaves
- Flowers
- Gardens
- Hoses
- Nests
- Trowels
- Baskets
- Sidewalks

PATTERNS

Use the listed objects to discover patterns. Also use these objects and have children copy and/or extend basic patterns.

- Flowers
- Gardens
- Vases
- Calendars
- Vegetables
- Clouds
- Clothing
- Bouquets

MEASUREMENT

Use the objects as standard and non-standard measurement for time, length, temperature, and weight. Discuss how some are used as tools and talk about their function.

- String
- Watering can
- Funnels
- Depressors
- Trees
- Magnifying glass
- Rulers
- Sticks
- Measuring cups
- Cuttings
- Twigs
- Jars
- Spoons
- Plants
- Spray bottles
- Bushes

SUMMER

Number
Games at the Fair

In the summer, children often have to devise games or pretend situations in order to entertain themselves. Their make-believe play often mirrors events they have recently seen, such as a fair, agricultural or pet show, vacation or fishing trip, picnic or barbecue. Many times, these activities involve using various mathematical skills--sometimes using more than one skill at the same time.

Plan a classroom fair with children. Provide them with some clear plastic containers and some type of counters—seeds or marbles. Ask them to invent a guessing game for the fair that will involve the containers, counters, and counting. Children may decide on a throwing game where the players can count how many objects can be tossed into the container or they may suggest putting a number of objects in that container, letting the people in the rest of the group guess how many are there, and then, counting the contents to see whose guess came the closest to the right number.

Reasoning
Fishing at the Fair

As children enter into dramatic play at your fair, point out some of the vocabulary involved and compare each new term with something with which they are already familiar. Help children realize that the same types of activities can be used in both situations, such as fishing in a pond and "fishing" at a fair.

Make a fishing rod out of a stick by attaching a string at one end. Fasten a magnet to the lower end of the string. Make different colored fish and attach a paper clip to the nose of each one. Have several baskets for the caught fish to be placed into, one for each color. Name the different parts of the fishing equipment—rod, line (string), bait (magnet). Let different children go fishing and see how well they land their fish and place them in the proper container.

Shapes
Where Does the Beanbag Go?

Children need to know more about shapes and why certain ones are used at times, and why others are not used. It is helpful for them to experiment with or make different shapes for use in similar activities, such as below and BLOWING BUBBLE SHAPES.

Have each child draw the outline of a big shape in the top of a cardboard box. Work to have the group include all the different shapes they have learned so far. Cut each shape out if you think children will have difficulty doing so, and put the shapes aside. (They can be used as patterns for other shape activities.) Prop up the box lids so that children can try to throw a bean bag through their shape space. After each child has had one try, move the lids back slightly and let them try again. Continue this process for several more times. Discuss with children through which shape space it is easier to toss the bean bags. Let them try throwing bean bags through the shapes that others have made. Make similar targets, but have the holes smaller. Let them experiment with distance and shape.

BLOWING BUBBLE SHAPES

paper cup

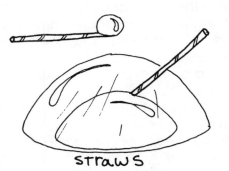
straws

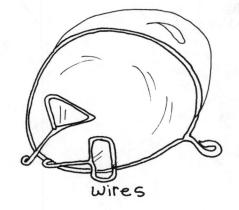
wires

YOU'LL NEED:

 water

 dishwashing liquid

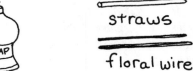 straws / floral wire

 paper cups

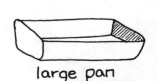 hanger

large pan

WHAT TO DO:

 1. With children's help, mix bubble solution as follows:

6 ounces water
1 ounce dishwashing liquid.

 2. Prepare bubble blowing tools:
- plain, plastic drinking straws,
- straws with one tip cut at an angle,
- heavy floral wire bent into a circle,
- paper cup with a hole punched in bottom.

 3. Have children dip each of these tools into bubble solution and blow bubbles. Have them describe shapes of bubbles.

 4. Help children bend more floral wire into differently shaped blowing tools—▲ ■ ▰. Have children blow bubbles and describe the bubble shapes.

 5. Bend a wire coat hanger into shapes—● ▲ ▰. Dip into large pan with bubble solution. Discuss shape of bubbles blown.

 6. Spread some bubble solution on a table top. Have children use plain straws to blow half bubbles on table. Straws should be <u>wet</u>. Have them blow bubbles inside bubbles.

SUMMER

Patterns
Listen While I Jump

Patterns occur in all sorts of places, such as in food—FRUIT KABOBS—or another area with which children are familiar—music. They sense the measured beats and the rhythmical patterns without realizing the strict adherence to a certain time. Rhythm cards, using vertical lines to represent half notes and horizontal lines for whole notes, can be made up for different songs. Then, children can see the musical pattern easily as they sing or play rhythm instruments.

Present some of the following jump rope rhymes and let children put them to music and jump according to the rhythm.

> *Teddy Bear, Teddy Bear, Turn around;*
> *Teddy Bear, Teddy Bear, Touch the ground.*
> *Teddy Bear, Teddy Bear, Show your shoes;*
> *Teddy Bear, Teddy Bear, Read the news.*
>
> *Charlie over the water, Charlie over the sea,*
> *Charlie catch a bluebird, Can't catch me.*

Let children make up tempo patterns as they play with drums or other rhythm instruments.

Measurement
Feed the Elephants

Children need to learn to estimate distances because so many of the games they will play later on require the accurate placement of objects in a distant, specified place. This estimation ability comes after a lot of practice.

Set up a "Feed the Elephants at the Fair" game by placing five containers along one line. Give each child five peanuts and let them try tossing each peanut in a different container. Let children mark off where they will stand by using their age—if they are three, they will walk three of their feet away; if they are four, the distance will be four footsteps away. (If children hit all the "feedbags," let them try one footstep farther back.)

Higher-Level Thinking
What Will Turn Up?

One of children's important thinking skills is predicting the possible outcomes of various situations. In mathematics, children are asked often to consider the probability of certain events reoccuring and in what type of pattern. Two of the easiest mathematical predicting tools to use are a square die on which a different amount of dots have been placed on each side and a coin. (With the latter, children can guess which side will turn up when the coin is tossed.)

Make your own paper die or use a foam cube. Make each side a different color, using paints on the paper die or food coloring on the foam die. Prepare a chart with columns that show each one of the colors on the die. Have children play a "tossing" game at the fair by asking them to guess which color will land on top before they toss. On the chart, indicate their guesses and put a little mark under each guess if the die landed as was stated.

FRUIT KABOBS

YOU'LL NEED:

 fresh fruits (you slice them)

plastic drinking straws

 Straws

WHAT TO DO:

1. Adult places sliced and whole fruits out on a dish for children. Demonstrate how each fruit can be pushed onto the straw. Discuss that kabobs can be made in patterns.

apple wedges

banana slices

whole strawberries

melon chunks

2. Have child place 6 to 8 pieces of fruit on straws in repetitive patterns that they choose. Young children should use only two types of fruits.

strawberry apple•strawberry apple•strawberry apple

melon melon banana banana•melon melon banana banana

3. For older children, suggest that they use all four fruits to make patterned kabobs or that they have 3 fruits in each pattern and repeat that.

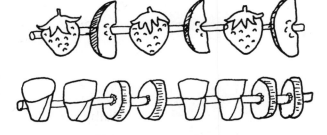

apple banana apple • apple banana apple

strawberry apple melon banana • strawberry apple melon banana

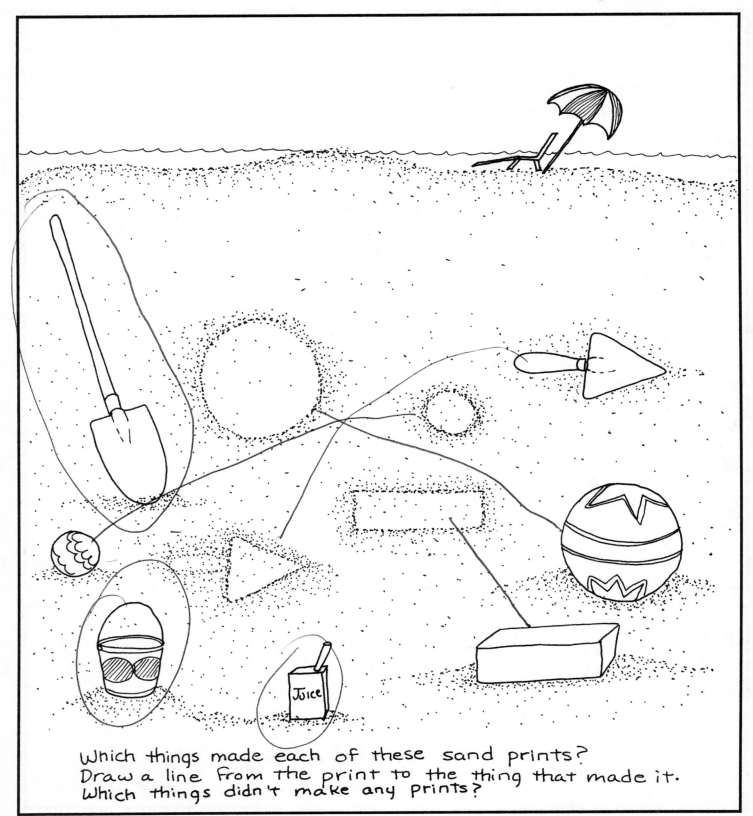

Which things made each of these sand prints?
Draw a line from the print to the thing that made it.
Which things didn't make any prints?

PRINTING

Which dolls made each of these sand prints?
Draw a line from the print to the doll.

SUMMER

DISCOVERY TIME

In summertime, children feel freer to explore, to dream up new activities, and to figure out solutions. They need to have new materials to work with so they can reach for higher goals and more mature understandings. You may want to include a nearby playground as a further place to explore. Below are some of the materials that you might have available to encourage their creativity.

NUMBER

Use these following objects as counters and as objects to be added to, subtracted from, multiplied, and divided.

- Tools
- Paintbrushes
- Nails
- Rocks
- Marbles
- Clothespins
- Seeds
- Buttons
- Band instruments
- Corks
- Clips
- Jars
- Coins
- Spools
- Counting games
- Bean bags

REASONING

Use these objects to sort by size, shape, color, texture, and by function.

- Baskets
- Color squares
- Corks
- Fish
- Sticks
- Tea strainer
- String
- Sponges

SHAPES

These are examples of various three-dimensional shapes. or materials that can be used to recreate shapes. Each can be used to discuss the basic shape and function of the item .

- Wire
- Containers
- Funnel
- Tent
- Sand
- Dirt
- Ping Pong balls
- Seesaw
- Clay
- Paper
- Wedge
- Wading pool

PATTERNS

Use these objects to help children discover and discuss patterns. They can be used as a basis for recreating patterns.

- Records
- Band instruments
- Paper
- Fabric
- Tapes
- Crayons
- Jump ropes
- Paper napkins
- Radio
- Paints
- Wallpaper

MEASUREMENT

Use these objects as items to be measured and for measuring.

- Sand
- Measuring cups
- Eye dropper
- Sprinkler
- Cornstarch
- Measuring spoons
- Ice cubes
- Swings
- Bubble solution
- Magnifier
- Rubber tubes
- Water table
- Watering can
- Thermometer
- Squeeze bottles
- Vases

SCIENCE
AND
COOKING

SCIENCE/COOKING

Reasoning
Which Is Mine?

This little game asks children to use their reasoning skills to draw conclusions. Set out two charts. On one, draw, in simple outline form, the following birds to approximate scale to each other: a hummingbird, a robin, a chicken, a goose, and an ostrich. On the other chart, draw the eggs that each of these fowl produce. The hummingbird's would be little more than a tiny dot. The other eggs would be scaled a little larger from the robin's egg (which in real life is about 1" long), with the chicken's egg next and then, the goose's egg until the ostrich egg (which would look like a softball if placed next to the ostrich drawing).

Help children think logically and guess that the smallest bird would have the smallest egg and on up to the largest bird having the largest.

Estimating
What Do You Think?

Use a chicken egg to demonstrate how heating or whipping an egg can change the shape, size and color of it. Before starting the next activity, have children make some guesses about what might happen. First, show the contents of a raw egg to the children. (You might want to tell them that the purpose of the egg is to protect and nourish the newly layed young of some species such as birds. Stress, however, that the eggs we eat do not contain baby birds. Only special eggs have that.)

Record guesses children make when asked how heat will change the egg. Do the same when they are asked about whipping the whites. Now demonstrate both processes and talk about the increased volume of whipped egg white as compared to un-whipped and how the cooked egg takes the shape of the egg-shell, as it will take the shape of any other container in which it is cooked.

Measurement
A Hard-boiled Look at Eggs

Time is the measurement that will be used for this activity. You will need a dozen eggs and a three-minute sand timer.
1. Set 11 eggs in a pan of cold water to cover and begin to heat, using medium heat.
2. As you wait for the water to begin boiling, open the one raw egg and show it to children.
3. When water has come to a rolling boil, start the three-minute timer.
4. When sand runs out, reset the timer. Immediately, remove one egg and open it to show children a soft-boiled egg. Let children taste eggs as they cook, if desired.
5. Remove one egg every three minutes and observe the changes until the rest of the eggs have cooked 18 minutes and are hard-boiled. Make Deviled Eggs with the six remaining eggs.

AS TIME GOES BY

YOU'LL NEED:

one, large jar

 8" square piece of paper (or pliable cardboard)

  SAND

 MARKER

watch <u>or</u> clock <u>or</u> timer

WHAT TO DO:

1. Roll the 8" square paper into a cone shape. Tape the ends securely to make cone sturdy.

2. With scissors, snip the point off the cone, leaving about a $\frac{1}{4}$" diameter opening.

3. Have child set cone into jar opening and fill cone with sand.

4. Help children time how long sand takes to empty into jar. Use only the amount of sand needed to make an even minute. Example: use only 3 minutes of sand, not 3 minutes 17 seconds.

5. Place sand in cone again and on the jar mark, with tape, the level of sand in jar at each minute as it flows down.

6. Use this clock: to time clean up, to time taking turns, for game times. Also, let children see how many things they can do in time sand flows - do puzzles, build with blocks, walk and so on!

SCIENCE/COOKING

Patterns
Step by Step

Recipes provide many opportunities for children to use their math skills. The most obvious are counting, such as "two eggs" or "eight servings," and measurement, such as "cups of flour" and "tsp. of sugar." Yet recipes also provide the valuable skill of sequential ordering. A recipe gives direction in a patterned order. Children learn that it is important to follow the steps, one at a time, from first to second, third, and on to the last one. We use the ordinal number names to describe the steps " first," "second," "third," "fourth," and so on.

Make this recipe with the children. Cook the eggs as suggested below. Use the sequential step terms along with a one -word description: "first, cook;" "second, peel;" "third, slice;" fourth, scoop out;" "fifth, mash;" "sixth, add;" "seventh, fill."

DEVILED EGGS
You'll Need:
- 6 hard-boiled eggs
- mayonnaise (enough to moisten)
- bacon bits, paprika, or parsley flakes (optional)

What to Do:
1. Cook the eggs as described below.
2. Place the eggs under cold water and peel.
3. Slice egg in half, lengthwise.
4. Scoop yolk out of white and place in a dish.
5. Mash the yolks with a fork.
6. Add mayonnaise to taste.
7. Fill the whites with the yolk mixture.
8. Garnish with bacon bits, parsley, or paprika, if desired.

Shapes
Shapely Sandwiches

Cooking and eating are two sensory activities. We enjoy the taste, smell and even the looks of foods. Children, in particular, respond well to foods that are pleasing to the eye.

This activity will enhance the appeal of good foods and develop math skills at the same time. Children will make fancy-shaped sandwiches with familiar fillings. Have children (or you) prepare fillings: egg salad, peanut butter and jelly, tuna salad and luncheon meats. Use cookie cutters, in heart, square, circle, and triangle shapes to cut slices of white or whole wheat breads. The cutters can also cut the luncheon meats. Fill the breads and cover with another slice. (You can use any shaped bread for any filling or you can use only one shape bread for one particular filling.)

What Do You Like?

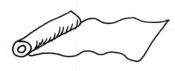

roll of shelf or brown paper

marker

ruler

children

1. With help from children, roll out equal lengths of shelf paper — one length for each choice.

2. Place the paper lengths on floor, parallel and about one foot apart. Make sure all paper lengths have the same starting line.

3. With marker, label each length, at the starting line with each of the choices children will make.

4. With ruler and marker, measure, with children helping, and mark equal sized blocks down each length.

5. Have children make a choice as to their favorite thing. (For example, sandwich fillings as described on page 72.)

6. Let children stand in one block, on their choice of favorite thing. Compare each choice and discuss the favorites.

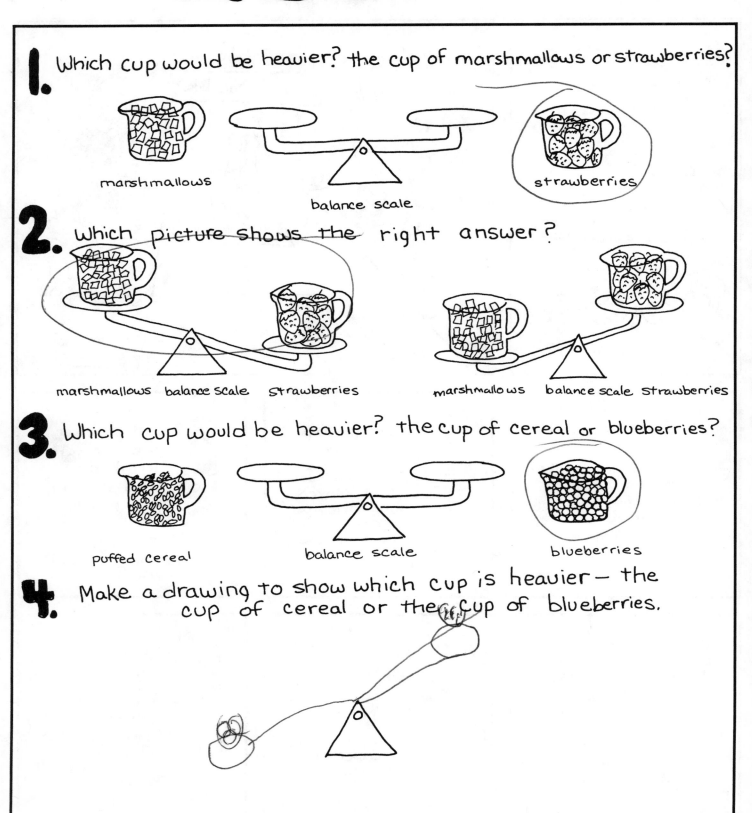

1. Which cup would be heavier? the cup of marshmallows or strawberries?

marshmallows

balance scale

strawberries

2. Which picture shows the right answer?

marshmallows   balance scale   strawberries

marshmallows   balance scale   strawberries

3. Which cup would be heavier? the cup of cereal or blueberries?

puffed cereal

balance scale

blueberries

4. Make a drawing to show which cup is heavier — the cup of cereal or the cup of blueberries.

BALANCE

5. Which cup would probably make this scale balance?

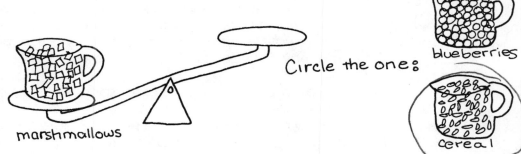

Circle the one:

blueberries

marshmallows

cereal

6. How many blueberries would it take to balance this scale?

blueberries

blueberries

Draw them in this cup.

7. You make this balance by adding some things to each cup. Draw the things in each cup.

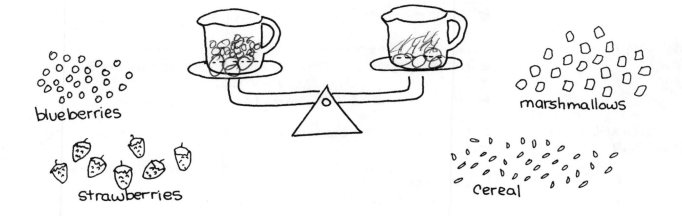

blueberries

strawberries

marshmallows

cereal

DISCOVERY TIME

Cooking is always a fun activity. Children are usually eager to 'help' and the final product is a bonus for them. But hidden in these special times are the math skills associated with reading and sequentially following recipes, doing the actual food preparations which include measuring and counting, and sharing the finished foods which often involve one to one correspondence and counting. Always keep the major math skill areas in mind as you cook. You may consider asking some of these questions:

NUMBER

■ How many (eggs, cups or teaspoons of something) does this recipe need?
■ How many people do we need to share this food with?
■ How many will this recipe make?
■ How many can work at this table at one time?
■ Do we have aprons for everyone that wants to help?

REASONING

■ Will all that food fit into this sized bowl?
■ Can we bake all these things on this one baking sheet?
■ Why does making a dough call for more flour than liquid?
■ What makes a pancake batter different than this bread dough?

SHAPES

■ How can we cut this food so that everyone has an equal sized piece?
■ Which cookie cutters will make the best cookies for our holiday meal?
■ Shall we make a round or square layer cake?
■ Where should the cooking tools be put back? (when outlines of each are drawn on the drawer or cabinet door)

PATTERNS

■ How can we set these different cookies on the tray so that they look pretty?
■ When making cookies what do we always have to do first?

MEASUREMENT

■ How much is one handful equal to in this measuring cup?
■ Find two apples that are about the same size for our recipe.
■ How much milk does this recipe call for?
■ Get the measuring tools we'll need for this recipe.

RECORDING AND USING INFORMATION

■ Let's make a picture recipe for the food we will make (or have made).
■ Let's find out who likes what kind of sandwiches before we make any.
■ Make a cookbook of all our recipes.

COLORS

COLORS

Number
What Color Do You Use a Lot?

Colors and numbers go together. Children make one yellow sun; they draw one green or brown tree and on that, they add any number of green or other colored leaves. When children create a rainbow with different colors of fingerpaint, they notice the effect of "adding" one color to another.

Let each child decide which color she or he uses most often. Ask the group, *"Which color do you think is used most often?"* Explain that the children will help you make a graph so that they can count to find out the answer to that question. Use a graph displaying examples of all the colors. At the top, print the question "Which Color Is Used Most Often?" Have children each decide on the most used crayon and draw a pretend crayon that color under the example crayon. Then, have them count each group and decide which one has the most crayons in it.

Reasoning
Put Me in a Group

Attribute blocks are good tools for children to use to experience the fact that objects can be sorted in a number of different ways. (Use a set that includes differences in color, size, and shape.) Start with simple tasks, and as time passes, present ones that are more complex.

Display a set of attribute blocks that are alike except for color. You can give one of the following sets of instructions, depending upon the group's knowledge of classification skills:

1) Look at this block and find another one of the same color.

2) Look at this block and find all the rest that are the same color.

3) Look at all the blocks and tell how we can sort them into smaller groups (by different colors). Add blocks that are a different shape to the group.

4) Look at all the blocks and put all the ones that are the same color together.

Shapes
What's the Other Half Like?

Symmetry, the exact correspondence in size, shape, and arrangement of parts on opposite sides of a line, is an important part of geometry—the mathematical study of shapes. It is easy to show in two-dimensional shapes that one part of the figure mirrors the other half.

Give children sheets of drawing paper and help them fold their papers in half. Have available different colors of tempera paint. Ask children to use a color of tempera and make three sides of a box or part of a circle on one half of the paper, making sure that they start and end their lines on the fold. Quickly after the work has been completed and the paint is still wet, have them refold the paper, press down hard, and then place a heavy object on top to press down on the painted area even more. Let children later on open the paper, notice the similarity between the two sides, and talk about what they have seen. Children can do the same type of activity with more complicated designs.

Guess A Color

You'll Need:

one dozen cupcakes

frosting (confectionary sugar type)

spoon

food coloring (red is great)

12 small paper cups

What To Do:

1. Set out three cupcakes with frosting.

2. One cupcake has white frosting to which one drop of food coloring has been added.

3. The next cupcake has frosting to which ten drops of food coloring have been added.

4. The third cupcake has white frosting to which twenty drops of food coloring have been added.

5. Help children estimate how many drops of food coloring are in the frosting of each of these three cupcakes.

6. Record all the guesses or estimates children make about the number of food color drops.

7. Have children divide the remaining frosting into nine equal parts. Add one drop of food coloring to one part. Match this frosting to that of first cupcake.

8. Continue to add a few drops of food coloring to each portion and have children try to match the shades of original cupcakes.

9. Have children frost remaining cupcakes and place them between the original three in order of color variation. Discuss guesses with results.

COLORS

Estimating
How Many Drops Will it Take.

Art work is full of estimating because all artists have to make guesses when mixing paints, deciding where to put an object in a picture, or choosing how big to make a single item or a group of items in a picture.

Provide clear plastic jars, eye droppers, and different bottles of food coloring. Let childen decide how many dropsful they will need to add and mix to make a new color before they start to work. Have them check to see how close their estimates were after they mixed a color. Children can also make shades of one color, using white frosting, as in GUESS A COLOR, or by adding small amounts of white tempera to another tempera color.

Measurement
What Size Will This Frog Be?

When children are imagining what they want to make in their pictures or in their craft projects, they have to think about types of measurement and size relationships. If they describe their work, listen to the types of measurement descriptors they use. You may want to add some new ones to their vocabulary.

Explain to children that you are going to give them special directions as they work with their art materials. Give instructions such as the following: *"Make a big blue pond at the bottom of the paper. Put a tall brown tree with green leaves by the pond. Make a short brown bush by the tree. Have a small black rock in the pond. Put a little green frog on the rock. Put a long red boat in the pond."* Let children show their pictures to each other so they can see how each one "defined" the various measurement words as they colored.

Higher-Level Thinking
Mix and Match

Children are using higher-level thinking during their work and play; it is just not occurring in an organized way. They show number relationships when they take ten markers and divide them in different ways to sort them into two containers. Then, they also can demonstrate the associative property of addition when they are mixing colors because the order in which the paints are added makes no difference in the final color. This can be shown both with the activity below and with the STRAW BLOWING.

Have three different bottles of food coloring, an eye dropper, and some clear bottles available. Arrange the food coloring bottles in a certain order. Give a child the eye dropper and ask that child to take three drops from each jar and place each amount in the same clear bottle and then mix them together. Rearrange the order of the colored bottles and have the same child or another one do the task again, placing the amounts in a second empty jar. Have the group compare the color of the two mixtures. Rearrange the food coloring jars again to a completely different order than shown before, and have the same steps followed after providing another clear empty jar.

STRAW BLOWING

YOU'LL NEED:

posterpaints in red, yellow, blue

straws

paper

WHAT TO DO:

1. Place three blobs of paint — one of each color — on each child's paper.

2. Have child use a straw to blow air over blobs of paint in order to spread and mix the colors. (Children should not touch straws to paint.)

3. Colors will blend forming oranges, greens, purples, and browns. Discuss the fact that it doesn't matter which color blends with which color.

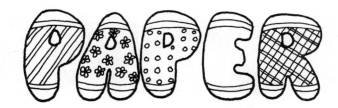

1.

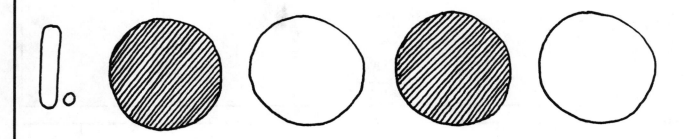

2.

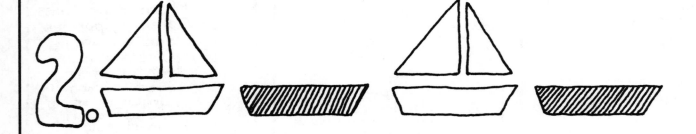

3.

4.

Make your own...

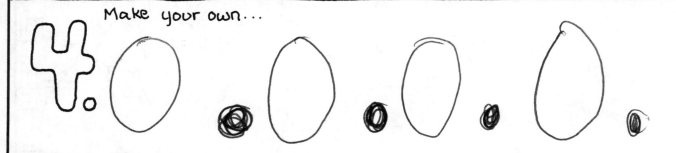

Finish each border pattern and then make up one of your own.

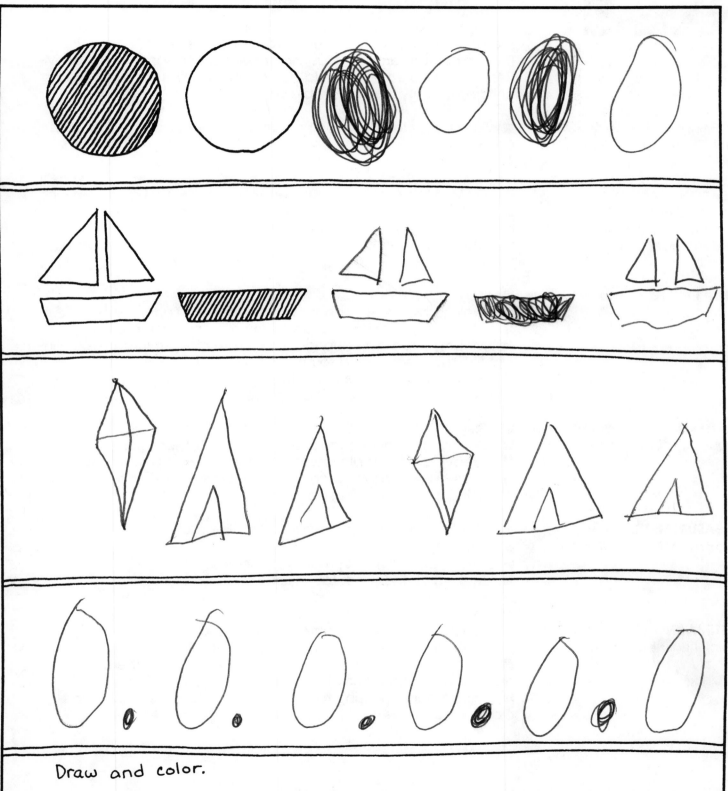

Draw and color.

COLORS

DISCOVERY TIME

The ART AREA provides many opportunities for children to use mathematics as they create all types of works of art. Below are the major math areas in *Counting on Math* and some of the activities in the art area that would be especially helpful in expanding children's ability to solve problems.

NUMBER (*"What will I do first?" "How many things will be in this?"*)

■ Making pictures with paints, crayons, chalk, collage materials, and so on
■ Sponge painting

REASONING (*"What kind of material will I use?" "What belongs in a picture about this subject?"*)

■ Making pictures of themselves with crayons, paints, and so on
■ Sorting objects in boxes of paint scraps, broken crayons or chalk, beads, paint chips, and so on
■ Making puppets with paper bags, fabric, construction paper, feathers, buttons, yarn

SHAPES (*"What shape will this turn out to be?"*)

■ Building with boxes
■ Making two-dimensional shapes with yarn, fingerpaints, sponges, scraps of paper, pipe cleaners, or paper plates
■ Making three-dimensional shapes with clay, styrofoam, aluminium foil, snow, sand, and so on
■ Making logos for people, classroom, or school
■ Cutting folded objects from paper

PATTERNS (*"In what order will I put the objects?"*)

■ Stringing beads or buttons
■ Sponge printing with two or three different sponges
■ Weaving with simple looms or making woven place mats
■ Finger painting with such accessories as combs and craft sticks
■ Stringing jewelry using pasta

MEASUREMENT (*"How much do I need?" "Will this fit?"*)

■ Making things using natural objects like rocks or shells
■ Stringing beads
■ Mixing paint in jars or making their own fingerpaint
■ Making clothes from fabric scraps
■ Preparing yarn or thread or strips of paper for weaving

ESTIMATING (*"How much do I think I will need to make what I want?"*)

■ Weaving or making patterns, figuring out about how much string or yarn to get
■ Modeling with clay, snow, or sand, figuring out if there is enough or too much or whether something will collapse
■ Mixing paints or using food coloring to make new colors, deciding what is missing

CHILDREN'S LITERATURE

CHILDREN'S LITERATURE

Number
Does a Picture Help?

Many teachers have realized that children must make the leap from working with concrete materials to the abstract thinking required by higher-level mathematics. They discovered that picture books are excellent stepping stones along the way. These often show many of the concepts involved in simple, fun, attention-drawing ways. Number, or "counting" books abound. Pick one, show how to use it, and then let the children enjoy. They can make their own number books, using the BIRTHDAY PARTY BOOK.

Pick a book, such as *Anno's Counting Book* by Mitsumasa Anno or *Helen Oxenbury's Numbers of Things* by Helen Oxenbury, and let children help you count the objects in the pictures as the story unfolds or the pages are turned. Have various children touch each object as its number name is said. This will help them make the connection between the name and the amount. Then, ask them to tell how many of an object are there. When objects in the book can also be found in the room, let someone bring over the same amount. Have the group recount both the concrete objects and the pictured ones.

Reasoning
How Can You Figure Out the Answer?

Books that ask questions and encourage children to figure out answers start their thinking juices flowing freely. Let them respond with any solutions they think of and explain how they decided upon their answers. Remember that each response is important because that child had a reason for what he or she said. Mathematical reasoning often concerns a person's recognizing what belongs to different groups.

Use Tana Hoban's *Is It Red? Is It Yellow? Is It Blue?* so children can sort objects by color. The book *How Far Is Far?* by Alvin Tresselt will stimulate a discussion about how to sort using various measures. Take any concept book, such as *Shapes and Things* by Tana Hoban, and ask, *"How are these objects alike?"* *"What is different about these objects?"* Then, discuss the category to which they are a part of by using the question *"What is the name of the group to which all these objects belong?"* It is always helpful afterward if children can take actual examples of what is pictured and move them together to show the members of a particular group.

Patterns
What Comes Next?

When children look around their environments to find the order in which events or objects occur, they are seeing patterns. As children are better able to realize that certain events happen in a consistent order or pattern each time, they find it easier to make predictions about what might happen later; knowing this information enables them often to solve new problems. Remember that time order, number order, and "design" order are all patterns.

Let children count the various groupings of legs in *Two, Four, Six, Eight: A Book About Legs* by Ethel and Leonard Kessler. One of the number books suggested above can also be used to talk about "counting" order.

BIRTHDAY PARTY BOOK

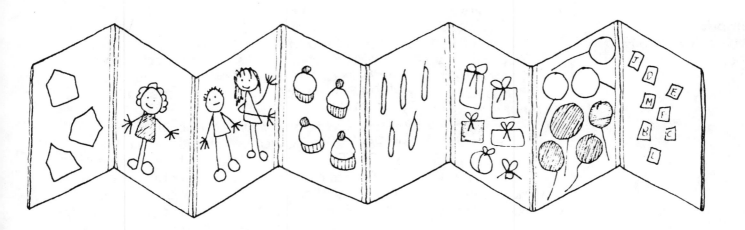

YOU'LL NEED:

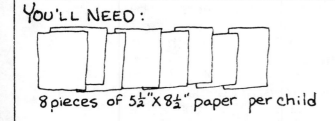

8 pieces of 5½" X 8½" paper per child

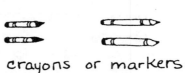

crayons or markers

transparent tape

WHAT TO DO:

1. Give children one piece of paper at a time. On the first piece, ask them to draw ONE birthday child. (Of course, this child could be themselves.)

2. On the second piece, have them draw TWO friends. On the third piece, have them draw THREE invitations.

3. On the fourth piece, have them draw FOUR cupcakes. On the fifth piece, have them draw FIVE candles.

4. On the sixth piece, have them draw SIX presents. On the seventh piece, have them draw SEVEN balloons.

5. The last page has EIGHT take-home goodie bags. Children now create their own birthday party story and book. Book can be assembled in any order.

6. Use tape to tape pages side-by-side (as a fold-out book) in order children like to tell the story.

Variation: Assemble in 1-2-3 order for simple counting book.

87

CHILDREN'S LITERATURE

Shapes
Where Can You Find Shapes?

The world is full of shapes, and children can find out about many of the shapes and where they can be found through the magic of picture book illustrations. Books can be used to show pictorial representations of actual objects and the groups to which they belong. This is especially helpful when items are not present in the children's environment.

Use a book such as *Round and Square* by Robert Allen or marcia Brown's *Listen to a Shape* to talk about simple shapes likes circles and squares. Let children draw pictures of the shapes or find objects in the room that are similar. Children can use paper or clay to construct what they think each shape is like. With a book like *What Shape Is It?* by Charles Hatcher, children can be encouraged to do more sorting and grouping of shapes. Making their own BOOK OF SHAPES will also add to their knowledge.

Measurement
The Sizes of the World

Children are fascinated by the measurement of objects in their lives because they expect exactness— *"How big is big?"*—and it isn't there. They don't realize that the size of each object depends upon to what it is being compared. When we are able to explain exact terms—which comes later—children will get a better sense of the length, depth, weight, volume, or passage of time of things in their daily lives. For now, pictures will help them better understand measurement concepts.

Is It Larger? Is It Smaller? by Tana Hoban can be read and discussed. Then, let children pick two similar objects that differ only in size and have a child point to one of the objects and ask the group the title questions. With a book like Rolf Myller's *How Big Is a Foot?*, distance measures can be discussed. Then, have children use nonstandard measures—how many hands long is that book— rather than regular rulers to measure actual objects in the room.

Higher-Level Thinking
What's Your Guess?

Young children should estimate, predict probabilities, and try to figure out what the unknowns are. There are books that will enable them to do so, a few of which are mentioned in this chapter. Find other books in which you can ask questions such as these.

- What's your guess about how many will fit here?
- What do you think will happen next?
- How often will this happen?
- How many more do you need to have enough?

A fun book that can be used for estimating and predicting is Pamela Allen's *Who Sank the Boat?* Help children make a simple boat or use some type of container and waterproof figures of the five animals in the story—cow, donkey, sheep, pig, mouse—in the proper relative size and weight proportions. Let them retell the story in its original order first, using a partially filled dishpan as their body of water. Then, let them experiment by changing the sequence in which the animals board. Ask them to predict what will happen before they place each animal on the boat.

BOOK OF SHAPES

You'll Need:

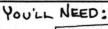

construction paper

 scissors

hole punch

 pencil

markers

metal rings

crayons

What To Do:

1. Trace and cut out many different sized circles, triangles, squares and rectangles from paper. (Older children can do this!)

2. Help children hole punch each shape with one hole and assemble shapes into a 'ring' bound book with a metal ring.

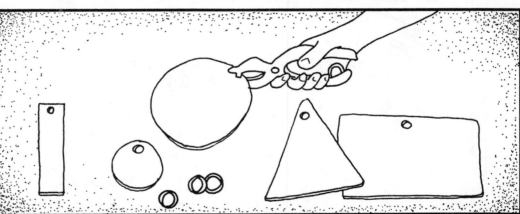

3. Give each child a shape book. Encourage children to add marker or crayon drawings to make each page special— using the shape as the base.

Find these shapes in the setting.

LAKE

CHILDRENS LITERATURE

DISCOVERY TIME

Here are some books that deal with mathematcs areas that you may wish to read to your group or keep on hand for children to explore.

NUMBER

Anno, Mitsumasa. *Anno's Counting Book.* Harper & Row.
____. *Anno's Mysterious Multiplying Jar.* Philomel.
Demi. *Demi's Count the Animals 1 2 3.* Grosset and Dunlap.
Kitamura, Satoshi. *When Sheep Cannot Sleep.* Farrar, Straus, Giroux.
Oxenbury, Helen. *Helen Oxenbury's Numbers of Things.* Franklin Watts.
Stobbs, Joanna and William. *One Sun, Two Eyes, and a Million Stars.* Oxford.
Tafuri, Nancy. *Who's Counting?* Greenwillow.

REASONING

Brown, Marcia. *Touch Will Tell.* Franklin Watts.
Hoban, Tana. *Is It Red? Is It Yellow? Is It Blue?* Greenwillow.
____. *Is It Rough? Is It Smooth? Is It Shiny?* Greenwillow.
____. *Shapes and Things.* Macmillan.
Tresselt, Alfred. *How Far Is Far?* Parent's Magazine Press.

PATTERNS

Clifton, Lucille. *Everett Anderson's Year.* Holt.
Kessler, Ethel and Leonard. *Two, Four, Six, Eight: A Book About Legs.* Dodd, Mead.
McMillan, Bruce. *Counting Wildflowers.* Lothrop.
Watson, Nancy Dingman. *When Is Tomorrow?* Knopf.

SHAPES

Allen, Robert. *Round and Square.* Platt & Munk.
Brown, Marcia. *Listen to a Shape.* Franklin Watts.
Emberley, Ed. *Ed Emberley's Amazing Look Through Book.* Little, Brown.
____. *The Wing on A Flea.* Little, Brown.
Fisher, Leonard Everett. *Boxes! Boxes! Boxes!* Viking.
Hatcher, Charles. *What Shape Is It?* Duell.
Testa, Fulvio. *If You Look Around You.* Dial.

MEASUREMENT

Briggs, Raymond. *Jim and the Beanstalk.* Coward.
Hoban, Tana. *Is It Larger? Is It Smaller?* Greenwillow.
____. *26 Letters and 99 Cents.* Greenwillow.
Lionni, Leo. *Inch by Inch.* Astor-Honor.
Myller, Rolf. *How Big Is a Foot?* Atheneum.

HIGHER-LEVEL THINKING

Allen, Pamela. *Who Sank the Boat?* Coward.
Anno, Mitsumasa. *Socrates and the Three Little Pigs.* Philomel.
Gag, Wanda. *Millions of Cats.* Coward.
Peppe, Rodney. *The House That Jack Built.* Delacorte.
Scott, William. *This Is the Milk That Jack Drank.* Addison-Wesley.

COMMUNITY HELPERS

COMMUNITY HELPERS

Number/Estimating
Where Will I Find 1, 2, 3?

As children pretend to be different types of community helpers during their dramatic play time, they will probably see different places where numbers and estimation are used. Encourage children to talk about the numbers and how they would use them.

Help children develop their favorite type of store. Have them decide how big to build the store, what to place in it, and what the cost of each product will be. Let them write the price tags, providing help, if asked. Have available some type of cash register and talk about the numbers given on it. (As children press different numbers on the cash register, let others press the same ones on a simple calculator.) Introduce various types of money—bills and/or coins or let children make their own play money. Have children take turns being clerks, shelf stockers, and customers.

Often a worker must guess "how much" in order to make a quick decision. The chef scoops up some flour to be put in a measuring cup; the gardner decides by looking where to plant a new row or the next plant. Let children portray different workers and make estimates in amounts, distances, and so on.

Reasoning
Let's Get Ready

Children will probably recall or figure out that the best way to get ready to open a store or to start any job is by placing similar types of materials or products together. Some may want to group by a general category, such as dairy products, while others may want to separate the larger group into more discrete areas.

Bring into the classroom empty containers of products from a food store or have children collect similar items from home. Have them make shelves using blocks and planks. Let children decide how many shelves they need by asking into what different groups they are going to sort their groceries. As children look at the containers that were collected, help them come up with the names of "big" groups, such as meats, laundry products, paper products, fruits, drinks, and so on. (It may be helpful to do the big group sorting before they decide on how many shelves they need.) After the shelving is ready, let children place the products on them by matching similar types of products.

Measurement
How Much Do You Need?

There are many careers where different types of measurements are necessary. Whenever a new career is being portrayed during dramatic play or being discussed, encourage children to think about and use the measuring tools that workers would need. For instance, have available some type of ruling device for gardeners or builders; measuring cups for cooks or chefs; balances or scales for storekeepers, postal workers; and so on.

Place different types of measuring tools on a table. Have a child choose one and talk about how the tool is to be used. Ask the group to choose a type of job or work where this tool would be used. Let children have turns pretending to be the suggested worker using the tool.

HOME BASE

YOU'LL NEED:

ball of yarn

non-standard measuring tools:
(many items of approximately same length and similar type)

crayons ^{or} pencils ^{or} brushes ^{or} blocks ^{or} paper clips

WHAT TO DO:

1. Cut yarn in lengths of: 6', 7', 8', 9' and 10'. Make enough so every child will have one. Let children pick one piece from among all pieces wadded up into a ball.

2. Each child makes his or her own 'home base' somewhere out-of-doors using the yarn as an outline of their space. Space should be enclosed. Set out non-standard measuring tools.

3. Children measure the distance around their home bases by placing non-standard measuring tools on yarn. Have children tell how big their home bases are in units they've chosen.

COMMUNITY HELPERS

Shapes
What Do Shapes Tell You?

Shapes also play an important part in the various tasks of certain community helpers. Sometimes, the shapes form part of the needed equipment, such as the round net that firefighters use; other times the shapes are used in the signs that a worker needs, such as the diamond-shaped highway warning signs. Since a number of different jobs center around keeping people safe, children should learn to recognize the meaning of the different-shaped traffic signs.

Take children on a walk around a nearby area where they can see different traffic signs. Talk about the shape of each sign and what that sign is indicating. On the eight-sided STOP sign, help them count each side, read the word, and do what it says. Show them an example of a down-pointing triangle (YIELD sign) and explain that drivers are supposed to slow down and be prepared to let other cars go. Let children see pictures of the warnings painted on diamond-shaped signs. Show them the round stop signs used by crosssing guards. Help children read the information given on rectangular- or square-shaped signs. Then, let children make their own signs and use the signs in their dramatic play as they portray different workers.

Patterns
What Patterns Are Needed?

All different types of patterns are used in the tasks of various community helpers. What children have to think about is what type of order is used as workers are preparing materials, following certain directions, or going about their jobs. Children are probably most familiar with jobs similar to those of a weaver, a cake decorator in a bakery, or a stock person in a supermarket where design patterns are used. Some may also know about the sequential steps used by assemblyline workers in a factory.

Let children pretend to be workers in a cafe or cafeteria in which they have to do several steps of a task in the same order for five or six times—such as putting play food on trays in exactly the same position or setting dishes and flatware on trays the same way.

Provide children with a round cardboard circle and ask them to design a sequential pattern for decorating the icing for a pretend cake. If possible, let them use some type of squeeze tubes with different colors of icing and actually form the pattern on the outer edge of the circle.

Mathematical Helps
Calculators and Computers

Children should become aware of the different machines that can be used in various jobs in order to make calculations. (Point out that people can do these same types of figuring but that the machines can do the work faster.)

Go around the school or to nearby stores and let children see how different workers use and care for computational machines. Ask if children can have experience with each, such as pressing a calculator or computer key.

CITY PLANNING

You'll Need:

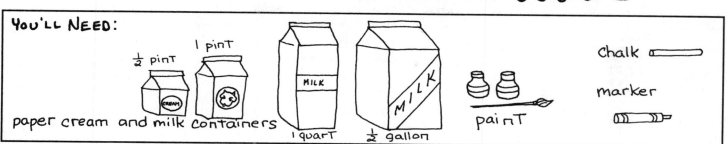

½ pint 1 pint

MILK

MILK

1 quart ½ gallon

paint

paper cream and milk containers

Chalk

marker

What to do:

1. Mark a space on floor about 2' x 2' with chalk. Have each child work on a section of this city.

2. Help child plan and estimate space needed to place milk carton 'buildings' in designated area. Have child pick the correct size carton for each area.

3. Encourage child to use estimation skills to determine how many 'buildings' could fit into an area. Complete each building with paint and markers.

COMPUTERS

Hilary

1. Write your name on the line on the monitor screen.

2. Color in all the Keys on the keyboard that are in the letters of your name.

CALCULATORS

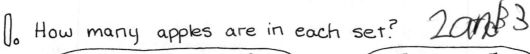

1. How many apples are in each set? 2 and 3

2. Color the keys on the calculator that tell how many are in each set.

3. Color in the keys that you will need to find out how many apples in all.

Write your answer in the display box, on the dotted line.

DISCOVERY TIME

There are any number of jobs that children might portray in their dramatic play in which mathematics could be an important part of the pretending. These workers would use skills from all the major math areas, but certain careers would lend themselves to really enhancing practical applications of particular areas. Below are the areas and some of the careers you might want to encourage.

NUMBER

Architects	Bankers	Carpenters	Clockmakers
Engineers	Librarians	Mail carriers	Pilots
Storekeepers	Teachers		

REASONING

Architects	Artists	Bankers	Carpenters
Detectives	Doctors	Firefighters	Gardeners
Judges	Lawyers	Librarians	Mail workers
Nurses	Police	Scientists	Storekeepers

SHAPES

Architects	Artists	Bakers	Carpenters
Cooks	Farmers	Gardeners	Scientists
Tailors	Teachers	Storekeepers	

PATTERNS

Architects	Artists	Bakers	Carpenters
Chefs	Cooks	Gardeners	Mail carriers
Musicians	Tailors	Weavers	

MEASUREMENT

Architects	Artists	Bakers	Carpenters
Clockmakers	Doctors	Druggists	Farmers
Gardeners	Nurses	Scientists	Tailors
Storekeepers	Weather personnel		

Possible equipment to have on hand:

Balances	Books	Cash registers
Compasses	Containers	Dials
Measuring devices	Sawhorse	Thermometer
Wheels	Clocks	Hoses
Tools		

CELEBRATIONS

CELEBRATIONS

Number
How Many Do We Need?

Any celebration requires a lot of consideration of "how many" because there are usually a certain number of guests that must be provided for at all times. There is the amount of dishes, silverware, chairs, parts for the games if each one is to have a piece, favors for each guest, and so on.

Help children play a version of "Musical Chairs" using a record player or a tape recorder. Decide on how many children will start the game and let the group count the players. Then, have the group count out the same number of chairs. Start children walking around the chairs and stop the music after half a minute or so and let each child try to find a chair. Remove one chair and continue the game. Have the child who doesn't find a seat start and stop the music the next time. Continue removing chairs and let each "loser" have a turn being the timer. Each time children find seats have the group count to see how many children are sitting in chairs.

Reasoning
What Do You Need?

Include children in the planning for some celebration. Ask them first to decide what "big" decisions need to be made in order to have children name the major categories involved. Then, help them break down those big groups into more specific details.

Have children discuss what elements of a celebration—type, invitations, food, dishes, silverware, entertainment, decorations—they think they will need to talk about as they do their planning. You might want to make charts with each major heading listed on a separate paper. Ask children to decide what members of each category they will need for their party and to try and find pictures of these items in magazines or draw pictures of them. If you are actually having a special day, let children get the real items in the right quantity and place them as needed in the room.

Shapes
Shapely Fun Activities

Games and dances are often started in different shapes—a circle as in the game "Duck, Duck, Goose" or a rectangular-like formation as in "Red Rover, Red Rover." Children can also make up their own game shapes.

Have seven children and two adults sit in a medium-sized circle. Have one adult hold one end of a ball of yarn and toss the ball to a child across the circle. Ask that child to hold on to a piece of the yarn and toss the ball to another child on the other side of the circle. Continue this process until each child is holding a piece of the yarn and the second adult is holding the ball. Have everybody continue to hold on to their yarn, stand up, and raise the "giant spider web" over their heads so they can see what small shapes there are in the web.

Start again and see if children can figure out how to make a big triangle or a big rectangle by tossing or passing the yarn ball.

BALLOON CLOWNS

You'll Need:

balloons · paper plate · cardboard · marker · glue · scissors · yarn · pencil

What to Do:

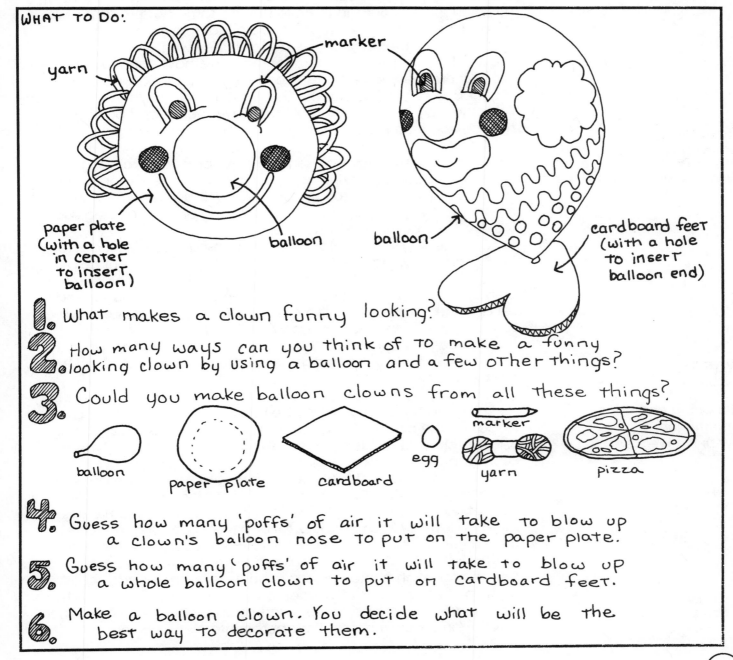

yarn — marker — paper plate (with a hole in center to insert balloon) — balloon — balloon — cardboard feet (with a hole to insert balloon end)

1. What makes a clown funny looking?

2. How many ways can you think of to make a funny looking clown by using a balloon and a few other things?

3. Could you make balloon clowns from all these things?

balloon · paper plate · cardboard · egg · marker · yarn · pizza

4. Guess how many 'puffs' of air it will take to blow up a clown's balloon nose to put on the paper plate.

5. Guess how many 'puffs' of air it will take to blow up a whole balloon clown to put on cardboard feet.

6. Make a balloon clown. You decide what will be the best way to decorate them.

CELEBRATIONS

Patterns
Look at My Mat!

Designing decorations for a celebration will bring out the patterning instincts of children, whether these decorations are for the room, tables, or individual places. Garlands hanging from bulletin boards, ceiling. windows, or doors can show patterned arrangements of Japanese lanterns, symbols of the day being celebrated, or other objects. Centerpieces and tablecloths may be decorated; children may also want to think about what to do individually for placements so that each one can develop a design.

Provide each child with a rectangular sheet of paper on which a border pattern can be developed with different colors, shapes, and designs. Encourage them to use the same pattern all the way around the edge of their mats. Explain that they can use the center as a part of their overall design if they wish. When children are ready to prepare the room for the party, have them place the mats where they desire to sit. Then, help them decide in what order each child will place the silverware needed for this occasion. After the work has been completed, have them stand back and see the continuous pattern of the silver on the placemats.

Measurement
Find the Right String

Children like to play games during celebrations, such as going on treasure hunts or looking for specific items. When trying to think up "things" for children to look for, items with different measurements can be used as treasures. (Estimating and comparing skills will also be brought into play.)

Cut one set of string into varying lengths, a different length for each child in the game. Cut a second set out of different colored string that are exactly the same lengths as those in the other set, and then cut a few extras of still other lengths. Place this second set and the extras around the room in different places, suspending some pieces using clear tape and laying others horizontally in visible locations. Give each child one string from the first set and have her or him find the matching length and bring both back to the circle.

Reporting and Using Information
What Do We Need to Do?

This math area will probably be used mostly in the planning stages for the celebration because using charts, lists, and graphs will help children make decisions about such items as the type of party, food, and working assignments.

Let children think of the different jobs that need to be done in order to get ready for some type of celebration. Have them help you set up a "chores chart" by letting them devise a picture clue for each job—balloon, for decorations; fork, for setting the table; record, for entertainment; orange, for food; ball, for games; and so on. First, have the group decide how many children are needed for each chore and show those decisions by adding that many pictures in the row by each chore clue. Then, let each child decide which chore he or she wants as an assignment. Write each child's name below one of the appropriate picture clues.

FOLDING FUN

YOU'LL NEED:

8" square papers · 6" x 11" papers · yarn · glue · scissors · markers

WHAT TO DO:

1. Have child fold 8" square paper back and forth in accordian style. Help them gather folded paper at one end and tie with yarn into a bow.

FANS

a) Fold

b) tie

2. Have children accordian fold a piece of 6" x 11" paper. Help them fold paper in half (see "b"). Tie securely (see "c"). Do not crunch paper where it is tied. Glue two open ends to complete circle.

FLOWERS

a) Fold 11" 6"

b)

c) tie securely

Fold

d) open and glue

e)

3. Have children accordian fold 8" square paper into 4 sections. Draw a "folk" person on front - make sure arms go to folds. Cut out and pull open chain.

FANCY FOLKS

a) Fold

b) draw and cut

c) open and decorate

TALLY-HO!

to a party we go!

Make a tally mark for each of these things you see in the picture. This is a tally mark: I .

CELEBRATIONS

DISCOVERY TIME

There are so many different opportunities for celebrating holidays, special times at school, individual accomplishments of a child. Each one offers ways of utilizing what children have learned about mathematics. Below is a listing of some materials and ideas. They are rather general because any more specificity would depend on the type of celebration that is being discussed. (Under REASONING, instead of listing materials, the general categories that must be considered are given.)

NUMBER

Calendars	Recipes	Guests
Shopping lists	Dishes	Silverware
Glasses	Balloons	Favors
Placemats	Napkins	Chairs

REASONING

Invitations	Food	Decorations
Shopping lists	Entertainment	Dishes
Games	Guests	Costumes
Gifts	Stories	Flowers
Activities	Music	

PATTERNS

Silverware	Dishes	Placemats
Tablecloth	Napkins	Decorations
Programs	Garlands	Flags
Cards	Stickers	Napkin rings
Chairs	Piano	Records/Tapes/CDs

SHAPES

Yarn	Dishes	Placemats
Garlands	Centerpieces	Napkins
Streamers	Name tags	Banners
Mailboxes	Ribbon	Japanese lanterns
Puppets	Ornaments	Flags

MEASUREMENT

Chains	Garlands	Streamers
Pennants	String	Yarn
Glasses	Ingredients	Thread
Dishes	Containers	Jump ropes

REPORTING AND USING INFORMATION

Lists	Charts/Graphs	Invitations

This is the science book you've been waiting for! This book is essential for teachers and parents of children two through five. Children learn by doing; they make their own discoveries, they do the experiments! You will be able to explain, through the material in this book, such difficult concepts as "air is almost everywhere," and "Water's weight helps things float." These and many other concepts are introduced through all the senses and in all areas of the normal Early Childhood curriculum--art, music, language development, and creative movement. The book emphasises the need to appreciate and conserve our environment, so that all can enjoy this Earth that we share.

NEW BOOKS from FIRST TEACHER

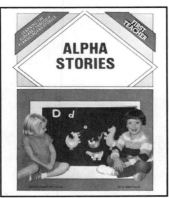

Here you will find 26 delightful original read-aloud stories guaranteed to captivate young children and reinforce the sounds of the letters of the alphabet. Each story emphasizes one letter and is followed by comprehension questions and enrichment activities to enhance the learning process. They expand alphabet learning into different subject and concept areas--from science and math to art and music. Also, there is a complete set of patterns for characters and props to be used on a flannelboard, which make stories more fun and encourage chidren to make up their own stories.

This is where you will find the best new mathematics activities for young children. Counting on Math encourages children to use simple mathematical skills to solve problems in new situations. This book provides hundreds of opportunities--games, art projects, recipies, music)al experiences, activities with books--for children to experiment with basic mathematical processes. This book is an invaluable resource since it provides a balance of activities from the entire field of mathematics--numbers, reasoning (logic), shapes (geometry), patterns, measurement, recording and using information (statistics), higher-level thinking--all within the normal structure of the pre-K and kindergarten classroom.

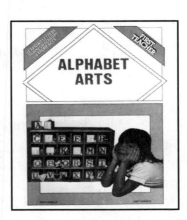

Unquestionably the best place to find more fun and educational activities for youngsters, Alphabet Arts contains over 300 exciting multi-sensory activities! Its projects, crafts, and games all introduce the children to the letters of the alphabet. There are 26 different kinds of crafts--from beadwork and applique to rubberstamp letters and pipe cleaner stabiles--all of which may be used interchangablely with any letters of the alphabet. Each craft is presented with full page, easy to read visual directions and is introduced by an individual story, poem, play, song, or game.

From the authors of **CONCEPT COOKERY**

CRAYONS
CRAFTS
AND
CONCEPTS

by

Kathy Faggella

Art activities can teach basic concepts and be integrated into the whole curriculum. Presented in one page, easy-to-read formats, that even your children can follow, these 50+ projects will fit into each theme and subject area, you introduce. There are also suggestions for setting up an art area, making smocks, safety rules, and follow ups for each activity. Projects are designed to be reproduced and sent home for follow up, too.

TABLE OF CONTENTS

- All about Me
- The Seasons
- Colors
- Shapes
- Language Development
- Children's Literature
- Celebrations and Holidays
- Science
- Opposites
- Math
- Feelings

Q: WHERE CAN YOU FIND HUNDREDS OF CLASSROOM TESTED IDEAS *EACH MONTH* TO HELP YOUR CHILDREN LEARN AND GROW?

A: IN FIRST TEACHER

Each 16 page issue of FIRST TEACHER provides you with innovative projects to make each day an exciting new adventure. We give you ideas for toymaking, games and recipes to do with young children. We take you to the world of make believe with ideas for drama and creative movement. And experts recommend the very best books for young children in FIRST TEACHER.

FIRST TEACHER has a newspaper format, but it's something to read and save. Each issue has a topical theme, so each one adds a permanent resource of projects and ideas to your school or center.

FIRST TEACHER is written by experienced caregivers, daycare directors, and nursery teachers, so it's full of tested ideas to help you guide and motivate young children

FIRST TEACHER has been read and used by over 30,000 Early Childhood teachers. Here's what one of them, Racelle Mednikow, preschool teacher for 16 years, says:

"What a pleasure to be provided with well written, resourceful and usable ideas that can be interjected into our everyday curriculum and be of true value to each of our teachers!"

"Thank you so much for this delightful, informative newspaper."

Subscribe today! Don't miss another month of ideas, projects, and activities.
